PORT OF
LEITH &
GRANTON

PORT OF
LEITH &
GRANTON

GRAEME SOMNER

TEMPUS

This book is dedicated to the memory of Derek Edminson and the many enjoyable hours we spent as schoolboys on the ferry-boats at Queensferry.

Frontispiece: Coal was once the staple commodity exported from both Leith and Granton but since the 1950s, as many local coal mines have closed, exports of coal have virtually disappeared. Here the coaster *Marna* (874grt, 1940), owned by Christian Salvesen of Leith, is loading another cargo of coal in the Imperial Dock, Leith, using one of several coal hoists and wagon traversers that were in service until the late 1950s.

First published 2004

Tempus Publishing Limited
The Mill, Brimscombe Port,
Stroud, Gloucestershire, GL5 2QG
www.tempus-publishing.com

© Graeme Somner, 2004

The right of Graeme Somner to be identified as the Author
of this work has been asserted in accordance with the
Copyrights, Designs and Patents Act 1988.

British Library Cataloguing in Publication Data.
A catalogue record for this book is available from the British Library.

ISBN 0 7524 3217 6

Typesetting and origination by Tempus Publishing Limited.
Printed in Great Britain.

Contents

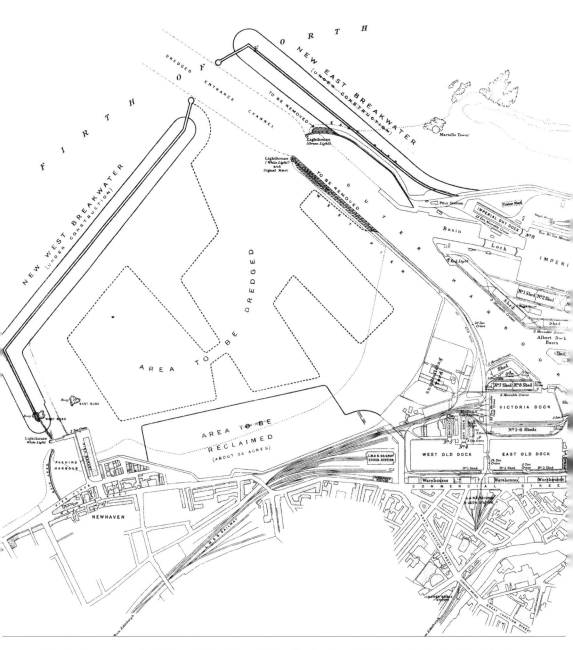

The dock system existed from 1904. West Old Dock, the East Old Dock (both closed in 1968) and latterly the Victoria Dock have now been filled in and development has taken place. Construction of a large new building which now houses the Scottish Office, on a site to the south of the Victoria Dock, was started in 1993.

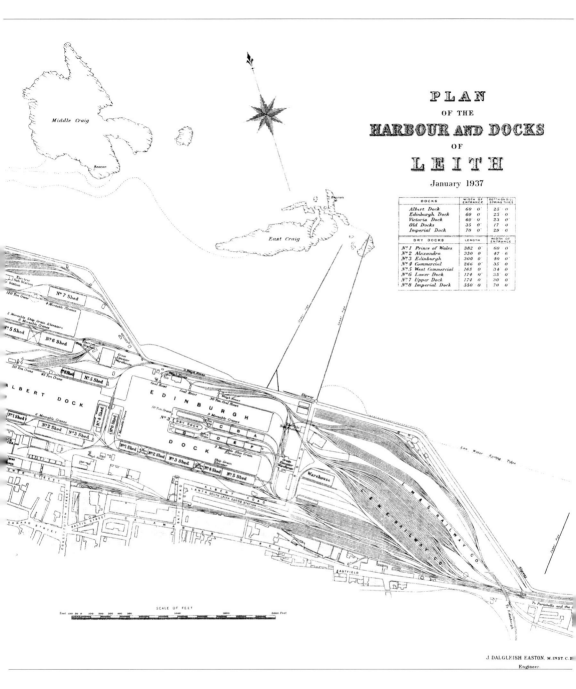

PLAN
OF THE
HARBOUR AND DOCKS
OF
LEITH

Janary 1937

DOCKS	WIDTH OF ENTRANCE	DEPTH ON SILL SPRING TIDES
Albert Dock	60' 0"	25' 0"
Edinburgh Dock	60' 0"	25' 0"
Victoria Dock	60' 0"	23' 0"
Old Docks	35' 0"	17' 0"
Imperial Dock	70' 0"	29' 6"

DRY DOCKS	LENGTH	WIDTH OF ENTRANCE
No 1 Prince of Wales	382' 0"	60' 0"
No 2 Alexandra	330' 0"	47' 6"
No 3 Edinburgh	300' 0"	40' 0"
No 4 Commercial	266' 0"	35' 0"
No 5 West Commercial	165' 0"	34' 0"
No 6 Lower Dock	174' 0"	35' 0"
No 7 Upper Dock	174' 0"	30' 0"
No 8 Imperial Dock	550' 0"	70' 0"

Middle Craig

Beacon

East Craig

Beacon

Electric Sub Station

No 7 Shed

2 Movable Ship Greas Elevators & Movable Crane

No 5 Shed

No 6 Shed

20 Ton Crane

42 Ton Crane

No 5 Shed

No 5 Shed

ALBERT DOCK

6 Movable Cranes

No 1 Shed

No 2 Shed

No 3 Shed

No 4 Shed

EDINBURGH

10 Ton Crane

No 3 Dry Dock

C B A

2 Movable Cranes

D E F

DOCK

No 1 Shed

No 2 Shed

No 3 Shed

Ship Grean

No 4 Shed

No 5 Shed

Canal Street

Coal House

50 Ton Coal House

North Wharf

Warehouse

ALBERT ROAD

LEITH SOUTH LEITH GOODS STATION

EASTFIELD

Low Water Spring Tides

L N E R RAILWAY CO

To Portobello and the

To Edinburgh

SCALE OF FEET

Feet 100 50 0   100   200   300 400 500   1000   1500   2000 Feet

J. DALGLEISH EASTON, M.INST.C.E

Engineer.

Acknowledgements

The majority of the photographs in this book come from my collection, which has been added to over the years. I started this collection around 1948, taking many photographs myself in both Leith and Granton, but also at other ports. I also purchased other images from photographers of that time. As the Scottish shipping trade contracted, so did the number of photographs added to my collection. Many of the sources of the photographs are only now known to the past, but to all those that stood and waited on various cold and windy pier heads to take the pictures, I am most grateful. I also am indebted to Captain John Landels of Dalkeith, the publisher of Tempus transport and industry books, Campbell McCutcheon, the Northern Lighthouse Board of Edinburgh, and others too numerous to mention, for the use of their photographs, advertisements and handbills in this publication.

Introduction

The Port of Leith

Leith, the seaport for Edinburgh, the capital city of Scotland, lies on the south side of the Firth of Forth. A settlement grew up in the twelfth century at the tidal mouth of the Water of Leith and by the eighteenth century, stone piers had been built out into the estuary. However, the major obstacle to the use of the harbour was the lack of deep water, caused by the existence of sandbanks at the river mouth creating a bar, which only allowed vessels to enter at high water.

Because of the lack of water at Leith in 1821 the first steamers for Aberdeen had to depart from Newhaven, a fishing harbour to the west of Leith, where it was possible to berth at most states of the tide. When that pier was no longer available the berth was moved to the newly constructed harbour of Granton, some two miles west of Leith, in 1840. In 1845 the authorities at Leith started to lengthen the East Pier, began to build a West Pier, had the harbour deepened by dredging and completed two small enclosed docks. By 1852 the East and West Piers were complete and a further dock, Victoria Dock, had been added.

These new facilities encouraged more established Leith shipping companies to introduce steamers onto their sailings. In 1841 the Leith & Hull Steam Packet Company (later to become the Leith, Hull & Hamburg Steam Packet Company) placed wooden paddle steamers on sailings between Leith and Hull. In 1850 George Gibson & Company (established 1816) brought into service their first screw steamer for their sailings to Rotterdam. A service to London had always been of importance and, while the London & Edinburgh Steam Packet Company (later absorbed into the General Steam Navigation Company of London) had run paddle steamers on the route since 1821, it was not until 1853 that the Leith-based London & Edinburgh Shipping Company (established 1809) introduced their first steamer. While these early steamers were introduced on the coastal and near-sea routes to

The 1906 view west from the Imperial Dock which was opened in 1904. The tug, appropriately named *Wrecker*, at the time the most powerful tug in the United Kingdom, is lying alongside the London & Edinburgh Shipping Company's *Iona* (1,242grt, 1883) and her near sister *Malvina* (1182grt, 1879). *Wrecker* was sold to foreign owners in March 1910 and *Iona* in June 1910.

Europe, it was not until 1871 that larger deep-sea cargo steamers were brought into service by local ship owners. William Thomson & Company (established 1839), later better known as the Ben Line for their sailings to the Far East, brought their first steamer into service in 1871. This was no doubt influenced by the fact that another new dock, Albert Dock, had opened in 1869. Christian Salvesen, trading to Norway and the Baltic, brought their first steamer into service in 1879. All these local companies were to expand over the years and bring prosperity to Leith. In turn, the prosperity of the port encouraged steamers from other ports to call there.

Further docks were completed in 1881 (Edinburgh Dock, 16½ acres) and 1904 (Imperial Dock, 19½ acres). By now regular services were in operation not only to Holland, Germany, France and Scandinavia but also to such far off countries as Iceland and Canada. The export of coal was on the increase and there was a continual string of colliers moving from the Forth to the river Thames carrying coal to feed the boilers of the electricity power stations and gas works in London.

The early part of the century saw many other companies sailing out of Leith. James Cormack, who acquired his first steamer in 1872, had grown from a one-ship company to a dozen ships, all trading to the Baltic. A.F. Henry & MacGregor, shipping agents since 1893, moved into ship owning in 1907 when they acquired the first of several steam lighters trading out of Leith and by 1910 with their larger vessels, had extended their operations to ports on the east coast of both Scotland

and England. This company was to trade for many years, carrying coal and stone from the Firth of Forth and the Tay to southern English ports, returning north with bagged cement from the Thames.

The outbreak of the First World War caused many shipping services to be withdrawn and found local ships locked up in German ports and confined to the Baltic. Many eventually escaped back to Leith. Other companies suffered major losses and did not survive the war. Russell, Huskie & Company, formed in 1892, was one such company that was wound up in 1917. John Warrack & Company, founded in 1874, went out of business just after the war. Thomas Cowan of Grangemouth, who first had placed a steamer on a service to Southampton and Tréport, northern France, at the turn of the century, sold the goodwill of that trade to the Dundee, Perth & London Shipping Company in 1919.

From 1919 trade gradually improved but only for around four years, as a steady decline then started. Companies built or acquired vessels to replace war losses but by 1930 trade depression had set in again and there were more ships laid up at Leith than there were trading. Again, some well-established companies ceased trading, with Richard Mackie & Co., formed in 1882 to trade to the Baltic, being one of them. Just as trade was picking up again, war was once more declared in 1939 and normal shipping services had to be abandoned. However, the unfinished Western Harbour site turned out to be of great use in the war effort and, in 1943 became the site for constructing sections of the Mulberry Harbour to be used on the beaches of Normandy in June 1944.

During the first half of the twentieth century, Edinburgh and Leith continued to expand and various schemes were put forward to improve the dock facilities, but no major works were undertaken after 1904. It was not until 1935 that Leith Dock Commission approved a new extension centred on the bay between Leith and Newhaven. A long breakwater extending out from Newhaven Harbour in a north-easterly direction and a short extension to the East breakwater extending in a north-westerly direction were approved, enclosing 250 acres of water. Because of the outbreak of the Second World War the Dutch engineers constructing it were initially banned from the docks area and the work on them slowed up. Eventually the engineers and their equipment, which had been requisitioned by the Royal Navy, were allowed to resume work again and the breakwaters were completed in 1942.

To enforce the regulations and to protect the fishing industry against inroads being made by foreign trawlers into Scottish coastal waters, the Department of Agriculture and Fisheries for Scotland operated a fleet of protection cruisers, many of which were based at Leith during their service. The cruisers were smart vessels painted in naval grey and flew the blue ensign with the department's crest imposed on it. The first fishery cruiser came into service in 1882. The first purpose-built fishery cruiser was constructed in 1898 and a string of other vessels then followed her over the years.

During the Second World War, many ships that docked at Leith regularly were lost, including fourteen owned by William Thomson & Company, and the London & Edinburgh Shipping Company lost its entire fleet of three ships between 24 February 1940 and 10 June 1941. This company remained in business, however, by buying the coastal company A.F. Henry & MacGregor and their fleet of eight cargo vessels in 1941.

After the cessation of hostilities in 1945, trade dropped sharply at Leith and the prospects of completing the new Western Harbour area seemed slim. However, two deep-water berths were constructed in 1952 to serve the new flour mill built in the area. Coal traffic was declining as the pits in the Lothian and Lanarkshire coalfields were run down and closed; even the opening of open-cast mines was only a short-term solution. Coal exports, which had been running at more than 2 million tons per year in 1913, had dropped to just over 400,000 tons by 1921, but had risen again by 1923, with half of the coal being exported going to England, Denmark, Finland, Germany and Holland. At the outbreak of the Second World War, the figure dropped to just over 600,000 tons and was not to recover afterwards. In 1957 it was only a little less than 400,000 tons and by 1962 it fell to as low as 26,000 tons. By 1960 there was only one hoist available for loading coal in the Edinburgh Dock (there had been three at one time). The forest of coal hoists once seen on the Imperial Dock quays had long since gone. The Far East trade had moved away from Leith and the new generation of larger Ben Line steamers now loaded at London, Hull or one of several Continental ports. General cargo being carried coastwise by sea was fighting a losing battle with road and rail services.

Opposite: An aerial view of Leith Docks. The vessels in the London berths (below left) are the General Steam Navigation Company's *Woodlark* (1,801grt, 1928) and *Peregrine* (938grt, 1921), and further to the right *Royal Fusilier* (2,187grt, 1924) lying alongside the loading berth of the London & Edinburgh Shipping Company, with *Royal Scot* (1,444grt, 1930) tied up at the discharging wharf at right angles to her. *Woodlark* and *Royal Fusilier* used to sail on Saturday afternoons for London, while *Peregrine* and *Royal Scot* arrived from London early on Saturday mornings, thus confirming the day was a Saturday. *Britannia* (623grt, 1918) on the Newcastle/Hull Saturday cargo service, is still in her berth above the Victoria Swing Bridge. In Victoria Dock (centre foreground), together with another of Currie's cargo vessels, is the passenger cargo vessel on the Hamburg sailings, the three-masted *Breslau* or *Coblenz* (1,366grt, 1882). *Royal Scot* came into service on 5 April 1930 and both *Breslau* and *Coblenz* were broken up in June 1932, so the photograph must have been taken between these two dates. By the angle of the shadows from various buildings, the time of day was late afternoon. It would appear, therefore, that it is a Saturday afternoon between 1930 and 1932.

Other vessels can be identified. Astern of *Peregrine* is the laid-up Glasgow-owned *Navarino* (5,103grt, 1907) – she was there for years! There is a tug alongside – probably the *Oxcar* (252grt, 1919). In the Imperial Dock the Cairn Line ships *Cairnmona* (4,666grt, 1918) and *Cairndhu* (5,250/1919) are laid-up. Registered at Newcastle, in normal times they would be trading to Canadian ports. In the Imperial Dock there are also three tugs, the two funnelled *Herwit* (256grt, 1904), *Flying Fish* (169grt, 1882) and the small screw tug *R. Nicholson* (200grt, 1891). Moored on a buoy in the Albert Dock are Currie's *Helder* (999grt, 1920) and *Helmond* (983grt, 1921), sister ships normally on the Baltic trade. There are fourteen ships in the Edinburgh Dock but because of the distance it is difficult to identify them, except to state that there are several large steamers laid-up there, including two further Currie ships. The large vessel on the south arm of the dock is one of Salvesen's whaling supply ships and there is also the small Coast Lines steamer *Pentland Coast* (423grt, 1915) in the south-west corner. In the East Old Dock (to the right) are a group of laid-up vessels. Nearest the quay are Currie's *Haarlem* (974grt, 1919) and *Stettin* (706grt, 1864). Astern of this group is the Fishery Protection cruiser *Norna* (457grt, 1909).

As well as trade dropping off, many of the pre-war shipping companies found themselves with changed trading patterns and rising financial costs. The London & Edinburgh Shipping Company joined with other companies to form the London Scottish Lines, chartering their ships to the new organisation, while fewer and fewer Ben Line ships called at Leith. The Leith, Hull & Hamburg Steam Packet Company had changed its name in 1940 to the more appropriate title of Currie Line with its trade to and from the Baltic being reduced, many of the ports of call there now being under Russian control. The North of Scotland, Orkney & Shetland Steam Navigation Company was now running a reduced service to Aberdeen and the northern isles because of changed working conditions on shore. In February 1971 they discontinued the passenger sailings between Leith and Aberdeen because of competition from rail and road services. The cargo sailings were finally withdrawn in 1990.

The London & Edinburgh Shipping Company continued chartering its ships to the London Scottish Lines until 1956, but as the charters were terminated, the vessels concerned went to the breaker's yard. London Scottish Lines withdrew from the trade in 1959 and sailings between Leith and London ceased. In 1963 the

London & Edinburgh Shipping Company sold its interest in the fleet of A.F. Henry & MacGregor to Christian Salvesen Ltd, as the pattern of trade had changed with the opening of Scotland's first cement works near Dunbar, East Lothian.

Containerisation in the 1960s resulted in surplus tonnage in the George Gibson & Company fleet, and some of their dry-cargo vessels were converted into liquefied gas carriers. The company ceased operating cargo sailings in 1969.

The end of 1967 saw the winding up of the Leith Docks Commission after 130 years, and in its place came the Forth Ports Authority in January 1968. The Authority took over the administration not only of Leith, but also of the ports of Alloa, Bo'ness, Grangemouth, Granton, Kirkcaldy, and Methil. A new entrance lock was brought into service in 1969 enclosing the whole of the port area.

The demise of the coal traffic was offset by a steel pipe coating industry in 1972. The pipes for use in the gas and oil industry arrived at Leith by sea and rail from various sources, and then had to be coated with a material to protect them from corrosion before being laid in the North Sea and elsewhere. The volume of traffic was to become quite considerable over later years, and it involved not only the landing of the pipes but the coating of them, before they were once more loaded prior to being placed underwater. This activity also resulted in a huge demand for iron ore concrete with which to coat the pipes, and this material arrived at Leith by sea from Scandinavia and Greece.

Improvements to the docks at Leith were implemented from time to time. A quay in the Albert Dock was altered in 1979 to accommodate the North of Scotland, Orkney & Shetland Shipping Company's ro-ro vessel which sailed weekly to Sullom Voe, Shetland, carrying materials for the oil terminal there. In 1982 improvements were made to the container terminal as traffic to Rotterdam increased. Nevertheless, Leith's shipping companies were on the wane. London & Edinburgh Shipping Company had not been ship owners since 1959, although they still managed A.F. Henry & MacGregor until 1963; Currie Line, whose conventional fleet had suffered as a result of the introduction of containers, was acquired by the Runciman Group in 1969 and passed to the management of the Anchor Line of Glasgow; George Gibson & Company also suffered the same fate, and although they had diversified into the liquid gas trade, they too were taken over by the Anchor Line in 1972. W.N. Lindsay Ltd, owners of coasters since 1932, went out of business in 1979, unable to compete with the low rates quoted by Dutch and German coasters. The remaining fleet of Christian Salvesen Ltd was now concentrated on coastal coal and North Sea trades, but it too suffered from competition and changed trading patterns, resulting in the company's withdrawal from shipping in 1989. Only Ben Line remained, with its head office in Edinburgh. For many years none of their ships had actually called at Leith and in 1993 they too withdrew from shipowning. There were now no major shipowners at the port.

Forth Ports Authority was privatised in 1992, which then allowed an investment and development programme to be undertaken. The port had suffered a long period of decline but is now undergoing revitalisation. The in-filling of the site of the Victoria Dock, together with that of the old East and West Docks which were filled in many years previously, allowed this large area to be developed to construct various buildings, industrial, office and private housing. However, the number of ships to be seen in Leith Docks today are few but the area is now thriving in a different direction: buildings are replacing ships and seamen. The noise of steam

The West Pier, Leith.

The paddle steamer *Lord Morton* (220grt, 1883) sets out from the West Pier, Leith, on another excursion, while the Grangemouth paddle tug *Blucher* (117grt, 1885) lies waiting for her next assignment, around 1905. On the outbreak of war in 1914 the tug's name was hurriedly changed to the less controversial *Dundas*.

winches and goods vehicles has now been replaced by the bleeps of computers and the chatter of people sitting in open-air restaurants and coffee shops. Summer Saturday afternoons, when many of the inhabitants of Leith (including myself) used to throng the jetty to see friends depart on the London steamer are no longer the same! Ships are fewer and there are no longer any regular passenger sailings from Leith.

Granton Harbour

Granton Harbour, situated about two miles west of Leith, was the creation of the Dukes of Buccleuch. In the early nineteenth century when there was dissatisfaction with the inadequacy of Leith, the Duke of Buccleuch, who owned the foreshore, was approached with a view to the construction of a harbour at Granton. The construction of the Middle Pier commenced in 1836 and opened on 28 June 1838. It was lengthened in 1844, providing ten berths, but had no protection from the winds blowing up and down the Forth. To give protection to the berths, construction of the West Breakwater commenced in the mid-1840s and some ten years later the construction of the East Breakwater followed. From the 1860s the West Breakwater was developed to increase the berths available in the harbour.

Ferry sailings across the Forth commenced on 5 September 1844, when a new

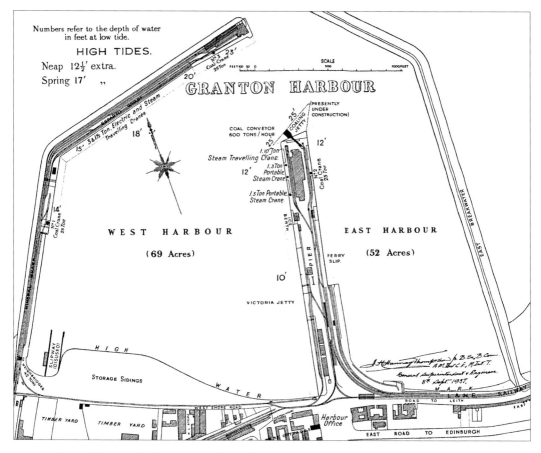

GRANTON HARBOUR

COAL CONVEYOR
600 TONS / HOUR

Steam Travelling Crane.

1.3Ton
Portable
Steam Crane.

1.5Ton Portable
Steam Crane.

(PRESENTLY
UNDER
CONSTRUCTION)

WEST HARBOUR

(69 Acres)

EAST HARBOUR

(52 Acres)

FERRY
SLIP.

VICTORIA JETTY

HIGH

STORAGE SIDINGS

WATER

TIMBER YARD   TIMBER YARD

Harbour
Office

EAST SHORE ROAD TO LEITH

EAST ROAD TO EDINBURGH

A plan of Granton Harbour at the time of its centenary in 1937. Some sixty years later most of the west harbour had been filled in and various trading and housing estates have now been developed on the area.

pier at Burntisland, Fife, was opened. The harbour was to see the first train ferry in the world in 1849. On the opening of the Forth (Rail) Bridge in 1890, the train ferries were withdrawn.

The railways first came to Granton in February 1846, which then allowed the transport of coal from the Lothian and Lanarkshire coalfields. Ships would sail from the harbour to England (especially London), Scandinavia and Baltic ports, not only with coal, but also coke, produced by the nearby gas works from 1902.

Both the General Steam Navigation Company and the North of Scotland, Orkney & Shetland Steam Navigation Company, regular users of Granton since the 1840s, transferred to Leith around 1880 as the facilities there were much improved, and their vessels were able to enter that port at most states of the tide. This was a blow to Granton but in turn certain Scandinavian vessels started making regular calls there.

In 1885 the first steam trawler started working out of Granton. The harbour was ideal, with deep water available at all but the lowest of tides, the facilities to make coal and ice on hand, with easy access to the fishing grounds in the North Sea. As the numbers of trawlers increased, they gradually took over most of the west side of the Middle Pier, lying there in banks of three or more vessels. The names of the local owners such as Devlin, Croan, Boyle, Cairnie and Paton became well known in the industry. The trawlers were small to begin with and only had bunkers for a few days, but as they became larger, with bigger coal bunker capacity, they made voyages of up to ten days. During 1936 over 3,000 trawlers landed nearly 11,000 tons of fish at Granton.

Incoming ships regularly brought in wood for use as pit props in the local coalfields, and esparto grass and wood pulp used in the manufacture of paper, and from 1909 petroleum products. As ships got larger, dredging had to be carried out to increase the depth of water. As tides did not have to be relied on, trade increased at a high rate, but this prosperity was halted by the outbreak of the First World War. The Admiralty first took over the Middle Pier (and latterly most of the rest of the harbour) as a base for minesweepers, themselves converted from the trawlers that used to fish out of Granton. It was not until 31 March 1920 that the harbour was handed back to the Buccleuch Estate.

In the years between the wars Granton prospered, with the export of coal increasing to such an extent that by the mid-1930s the three coal hoists already in service had to be supplemented by the opening of a new coal jetty as an extension to the Middle Pier in 1937. Colliers loaded more and more coal for the many electricity power stations and gas works in the London area. Not only did these utility companies own ships themselves, but to supplement them, they also employed vessels owned by such companies as Cory Colliers Ltd, their larger vessels being capable of uplifting some 3,000 tons of coal. During 1936 a total of 331 vessels sailed from Granton, carrying over 600,000 tons of coal and coke. The fishing fleet based at Granton rose to eighty vessels at its peak, which called for additional services to supply them with coal to feed their furnaces (oil fuel and diesel engines were still some years away) and ice to freeze their catch. The arrival of esparto grass from North Africa was also on the increase. The berths on the West Breakwater were improved and electric cranes installed to supplement the steam ones. A total of nearly 80,000 tons of esparto grass was discharged in 1936.

In 1932 the harbour became a private limited company although the Buccleuch family retained control. Ship repair facilities were improved by the acquisition of a small floating dock from the Admiralty. A second floating dock was acquired in 1947. A small shipbreaking concern was established in the mid-1930s by Malcolm Brechin in the west harbour, where small coasters and naval ships as well as many trawlers were dismantled, with the scrap from them being taken away by rail.

On the opening of the Forth Bridge in 1890, the ferry service between Granton and Burntisland, which had been operating since 1844, was greatly reduced and only the foot passenger (and the odd horse and cart) service remained. Initially two paddle steamers maintained these sailings but it was soon found that one steamer could cope with the traffic and one was withdrawn in 1892. In 1910 space was created on the foredeck so that a few newfangled motor cars could be carried. The withdrawal of the passenger train service from Edinburgh to Granton (the station was about 100yds from the pier) in the early 1920s did not improve matters.

The days of the ferry service were numbered. At the outbreak of the Second World War, Granton Harbour was once again taken over by the Admiralty as a base for minesweepers. Sailings continued until 20 March 1940 but were never resumed.

Parliamentary authority was finally given in 1947 to abandon the ferry service.

However, this was not to be the end of the ferry service. In March 1949 a new company was given permission by the Ministry of Transport to open a service, using four former LCT(4) landing craft. This proved not to be viable and the service was withdrawn in July 1952. The ferry-boat piers at Granton and Burntisland still remain, but no passengers now walk down them.

Another organisation which regularly used Granton Harbour for many years was the lighthouse tenders of the Northern Lighthouse Board. Initially the tenders were based at Leith, but in 1874 they were transferred to Granton Harbour. With the automation of lighthouses, a second tender at Granton was no longer justified and it was withdrawn in 1962.

The Second World War caused further disruption to trade at Granton. The harbour was taken over again as a minesweeper base, and all commercial traffic was excluded. When peace returned in 1945, coal exports were in decline, as at Leith, and although a new oil tank farm was built in 1959, which brought larger tankers into port, this traffic never made up for the short-fall in coal exports. The esparto grass traffic also declined, due to a change in the amount used in the paper industry, although Granton in fact still accounted for a third of the tonnage that was landed in the United Kingdom. For a time in the 1950s, vessels owned by J.P. Salvesen of Grangemouth and Christian Salvesen of Leith (the families were related) discharged cargoes of wood pulp at Granton. Many of the berths on the West Breakwater, previously used to discharge wood and esparto grass, were now occupied by the larger trawlers brought into service.

Despite the Depression Granton still retained its position as a major fishing port throughout the 1920s and 1930s, with the fleet numbering sixty-two vessels in 1928. In 1956 Granton saw the arrival of its first diesel trawler. By 1962, however, the number of trawlers based at Granton had dropped to just fifteen, and the fleet was in terminal decline. Devlin's, which at one time had the biggest fleet at Granton, laid up their last trawler in July 1962.

The timber wharves built along the West Breakwater slowly fell into disrepair during the 1960s and were gradually abandoned, the exception being the oil berth at the outer end which remained in use until the 1970s. On 1 January 1968 the Forth Ports Authority took over the management of Granton and the gradual rundown of the harbour commenced. Commercial traffic was almost non-existent by now and there was only the odd trawler based there. In 1970 a small grab dredger which had kept the harbour open for many years was sold and it was not long before the berths started to silt up. The harbour was closed to commercial traffic in 1974, and a year later the Northern Light Board's tender moved her berth to Leith. Trawlers, however, continued to land their catches at Granton until 1978.

Activity at Granton is now confined to the eastern half of the harbour, with yachts occupying the area. The western half of the harbour has gradually been in-filled and built on, although the outer part of the Middle Pier still exists. The days when there was a smell of tar (from treated fishing nets) and fish in the air, the noise and clatter of steam cranes working, and coal thundering into ship's holds has passed forever.

one

Coasting
South

The most important regular coastal ('liner') berths at Leith were those for London. From the early 1800s two companies had dominated the trade: the London & Edinburgh Shipping Company of Leith, and the General Steam Navigation Company of London. The London & Edinburgh Shipping Company constructed over the years a series of vessels specifically built for the route, with passenger accommodation. The early ships had only cramped accommodation under the poop for a small number of passengers, but by the 1920s over 200 passengers could be carried in style, with the first-class accommodation located amidships. Through most of the period, three sailings a week were offered by each company, and their berths at Leith were in close proximity to each other. By June 1941 the London and Edinburgh Shipping Company found itself with no ships as a result of enemy action. A cargo-only service was operated for the rest of the war, using ships allocated by the Ministry of War Transport. On the return of peace in 1945, with the coastal trade in decline and the cost of replacement tonnage being prohibitive, London & Edinburgh Shipping Company, the General Steam Navigation Company and various other companies operating between Scottish ports and London, came to an agreement that they should merger and operate a joint cargo-only service from Leith. For this purpose a new company was formed with the title of London Scottish Lines Ltd. However, the decline in trade continued as the result of competition from both road and rail, and in January 1959 the sailings ceased altogether.

Frequent 'liner' services to Newcastle and Hull as well Southampton and Tréport, in northern France, were also maintained by James Currie & Company and the Dundee, Perth & London Shipping Company respectively, but these services were for cargo only. The decline of trade also caused their withdrawal after 1945.

One of the early passenger steamers was *Malvina* (1,244grt, 1879). She proved to be a mainstay of the route for many years. Her end came on 2 August 1918 when she was torpedoed and sunk near Flamborough Head, Yorkshire.

Fingal (1562grt, 1894), built at Dundee, was one of the next generation of steamers to join the fleet. She too was lost by enemy action off Coquet Island, Northumberland, on 15 March 1915.

Fiona (1611grt, 1905) was also built at Dundee. She was a 'flyer' and was capable of a speed of 17½kts. She was requisitioned by the Royal Navy in 1914 and, while acting as an HM Boarding Ship, was wrecked on the Pentland Skerries, near Scapa Flow, on 7 September 1917.

Above: The London & Edinburgh Shipping Company's largest passenger steamer, *Royal Archer* (2,266grt, 1928), came into service on 31 March 1928 and took up the regular Wednesday sailings from Leith. She became a casualty of war on 24 February 1940 when she struck a mine in the Firth of Forth and sank.

Opposite above: The last ship built by the company before the First World War was *Royal Scot* (1726grt, 1910), with accommodation for 100 first class and 120 second class passengers. In 1919 *Royal Scot*, the only surviving passenger ship in the fleet, continued the service until 1930 when she was replaced and laid up at Leith. Sold in October 1932 to the Colombian Navy as a transport, she was finally broken up in 1946.

Opposite below: A product of a Dundee yard joined the fleet in 1924 – *Royal Fusilier* (2187grt, 1924). With accommodation for 148 first-class and 132 second-class passengers, she was an instant success on the popular Saturday sailings from Leith. She was attacked by enemy aircraft off the Longstone Light, Farne Islands, when bound north on 3 June 1940. Taken in tow, she capsized and sank at the entrance to the Firth of Forth, becoming a total loss.

Above and below: The General Steam Navigation Company did not build specific ships for their London sailings but allocated suitable vessels from within their large fleet, using such vessels (with limited passenger accommodation) as *Peregrine* (933grt, 1921, above) and *Woodlark* (1,501grt, 1928, below) to operate their service. It was not until after the Second World War that the two companies merged their services.

Initially London Scottish Lines chartered ships and from June 1946 *Belvina* (1,226grt, 1924), purchased by the London & Edinburgh Shipping Company in June 1945, was included. A typical coaster of her time, her size was ideal for the London sailings and she continued to carry cargo on the route until her arrival at the shipbreakers at Rosyth in February 1958.

Because of her good cargo capacity and handling facilities, *Belravock* (1,276grt, 1920) was also chartered by London Scottish Lines in early 1946. She continued on the route until June 1956, when the operation of a coal-burning steamer on a route that was in decline was no longer economical, and she went to the breakers at Rosyth.

The London Scottish Lines purchased their first ship in November 1946. Named *London Merchant* (733grt, 1935), she was to remain in service until the sailings were withdrawn in January 1959. Sold in April 1959 to owners in the Maldives, her end came on 28 June 1967, when she ran ashore off the Burmese coast near Cape Negrais, and was abandoned the following day. Her crew then had to made a cross-country march of several hundred miles to safety in Rangoon.

London Scottish Lines bought out a service between Leith and London, operated by the Scottish Co-operative Society, in June 1950. At the same time they acquired the motor vessel *Scottish Co-Operator* (513grt, 1939). She was renamed *Edinburgh Merchant*, and as the only motor vessel in the fleet, sailed on the route until her arrival at Leith on 13 December 1958, where she was laid up. *Edinburgh Merchant* was sold to Greek owners in March 1959, finally being broken up in 1975.

Currie's steamer *Britannia* (623grt, 1918), seen here in the Tyne, maintained a weekly service from Leith to Newcastle and Hull. Built as a patrol vessel for the Royal Navy in 1918, both bow and stern looked similar, in an attempt to puzzle any U-boat as to which way she was going. She had been converted to a cargo ship when purchased by Currie's in December 1923. She remained on the sailings until they were withdrawn in February 1940, and was sold for further trading in November 1945. *Britannia* was given an oil engine in 1957, and survived under an Italian flag until 1976.

Towards the end of the 1930s, Currie's had decided that new ships were needed for the Newcastle/Hull sailings and went as far as ordering a new motor ship. She was named *Edina* (489grt, 1939), but war intervened and she was employed elsewhere. Sold to Dundee owners in March 1946, twelve years later she was purchased by Caribbean owners. She foundered off Jamaica on 7 September 1964.

Another regular sailing was that to Dundee, Southampton and Tréport by the Dundee, Perth & London Shipping Company. *Louga* (952grt, 1898) had been operating the sailings for Thomas Cowan of Grangemouth on this route since being built, and the Dundee, Perth & London Shipping Company continued the trade on acquiring that company in 1919. *Louga* was sold to Lithuanian owners in 1937 and was wrecked in the Baltic on 15 November 1939.

The motor vessel *Lochee* (994grt, 1937), built at the Leith yard of Henry Robb Ltd, replaced *Louga*. Wartime found her in service in strange waters, and on 23 December 1940 she was mined and badly damaged in the river Mersey. There was no coastal trade for her to return to in 1945 so she was employed for some years in the Great Lakes in North America and general tramping. Sold in May 1963 to Greek owners, on 22 September 1979 she became stranded in the Red Sea after an engine breakdown, and was towed to Suez and laid up. She sank at her moorings on 1 October 1979.

two

The North
Boats

Regular 'liner' sailings to the north were a lifeline to many people, especially those inhabiting the northern isles of Scotland. The North of Scotland, Orkney & Shetland Steam Navigation Company, based at Aberdeen, had operated sailings to these isolated islands since 1790, first with sailings vessels, and then gradually introducing steam paddle ships to the services from 1826. The early passenger accommodation was very basic and it was not until 1937 that first class accommodation was located amidships (previously under the poop) and second class moved from the forecastle to the poop. Motor ships took over from the steamers from 1946. The 'North' company was taken over by Coast Lines in 1961 and, ten years later by the P&O. Passenger sailings between Leith and Aberdeen were withdrawn in February 1971.

Opposite above: A long-serving member of this fleet was *St Ninian* (702grt, 1895), seen here entering Leith on 20 May 1938. She served through both wars as a fleet transport at the naval base at Scapa Flow in the Orkneys. Laid-up at Aberdeen in 1946 she finally arrived at Rosyth to be broken up on 9 June 1948.

One of the early screw steamers (complete with clipper bow) was the iron steamer *St Clair* (567grt, 1868). She is seen lying at her berth at Leith on 28 April 1937, shortly after she had been renamed *St Colm* to allow her old name to be used by a new vessel. She was mainly employed serving Aberdeen, Wick and Thurso and did so for sixty-nine years until broken up in Germany in July 1937.

The slightly larger *St Rognvald* (923grt, 1901) joined the fleet around six years later. Although attacked twice by enemy aircraft in 1940 and 1941, she survived the war and was withdrawn from service in January 1951. She arrived at the breaker's yard at Ghent, Belgium, on 24 January 1951.

The first new steamer after the First World War was *St Magnus* (1,529grt, 1924). She was sent to Norway to assist British forces there in May 1940. Even in her last year of service she appeared very smart, as seen here on her departure from Leith in the summer of 1960. She arrived in tow at Rotterdam for breaking up on 30 October 1960.

St Clair (1,637grt, 1937) was the company's last steam ship when, by the amount of smoke, coal was obviously still king ! She was requisitioned in 1940, serving latterly as a convoy rescue ship. She operated the Aberdeen–Lerwick direct service until withdrawn from service in April 1967. She was broken up at Bruges, Belgium, later that year.

Summer Tours

To CAITHNESS ORKNEY and SHETLAND ISLANDS
From LEITH and ABERDEEN

By the New Steamer "St. Clair" and other First-Class Passenger Vessels

REGULAR AND DIRECT SAILINGS TO CAITHNESS, ORKNEY AND SHETLAND.

INCLUDING MEALS AND ACCOMMODATION ABOARD

	From LEITH	From ABERDEEN
4 Days' Cruise, Tuesday to Saturday	£5 10/-	£5
5 Days' Cruise, Thursday to Wednesday	£7	£6 10/-
5 Days' Cruise, Sunday to Friday	£7	£6 10/-
12 Days' Holiday—This includes 5 days' Cruise from Leith with a week's residence at ST. MAGNUS HOTEL, Hillswick	£12	£11 10/-
3 Days' Cruise to CAITHNESS, Monday to Thursday	£4	£3 10/-

ST. MAGNUS HOTEL
HILLSWICK, SHETLAND.

OPEN - - - - - JUNE TO SEPTEMBER.

Grand Rock Scenery
Bathing
Fishing
Motoring, etc.

For Full Particulars apply to

The North of Scotland & Orkney & Shetland Steam Navigation Co. Ltd.

Dept. B.10 TOWER PLACE, LEITH

Telegrams: "NORTHWARDS," LEITH
Telephone: 36471

OR TO HEAD OFFICE:
Dept. B.10 MATTHEWS' QUAY, ABERDEEN

Telegrams: "NORTHWARDS" ABERDEEN
Telephones: 2860-4 (5 lines)

This advertisement published in 1937 shows the clipper-bowed steamer *St Sunniva* (1,368grt, 1931), a replacement for the vessel of the same name wrecked on 10 April 1930. She was employed in the summer only on a weekly Leith to Lerwick sailing via Aberdeen. She was requisitioned in August 1939 by the Royal Navy and in December 1942 was commissioned as a convoy rescue ship. She was lost with all hands in the North Atlantic after her rigging became encrusted with ice, causing her to capsize, on 23 January 1943.

To replace cargo ships lost during the Second World War, the company ordered the motor ship *St Clement* (460grt, 1946), to supplement the sailings from Leith to Kirkwall and Stromness. With accommodation for twelve passengers, she remained in service until December 1976, when she was sold to Greek owners. She was broken up in May 1990.

The first major motor passenger ship was the twin-screw *St Ninian* (2,242grt, 1950), seen lying at her berth in Leith in 1951. Employed on weekly sailings between Leith, Aberdeen, Kirkwall and Lerwick, she proved very versatile, so much so that in 1970–71 she relieved ships on the Liverpool–Belfast sailings. On 26 April 1971 she sailed from Aberdeen after her sale to Canadian owners to undertake cruises from Halifax, Nova Scotia. However, that company went bankrupt and she was sold to South American owners in 1976. Her luck proved no better and she finally was broken up at Guayaquíl in 1991.

The motor ship *St Rognvald* (1,024grt, 1954) was built as a livestock carrier, and originally it had been intended to provide accommodation for fifty passengers. Ultimately this was reduced to twelve. She was sold in May 1977 to Panamanian owners for service in the western Mediterranean/Canary Islands until laid up at Las Palmas, Canary Islands, in July 1993. She was handed over by the Las Palmas Port Authority to local shipbreakers for demolition on 28 July 1998 – obviously someone had not being paying the bills!

Another milestone in the company's history was the introduction of the third ship named *St Clair* (3,033grt, 1960). She was built to operate the direct sailings between Aberdeen and Lerwick and demonstrated a huge advance in ship design. Her superstructure was constructed of aluminium, and she was fitted with anti-roll stabilisers – something long needed on this stormy route. Sold in 1977 to Kuwaiti owners, she was broken up in August 1987.

Above and below: There was competition on the route from Leith to Kirkwall from March 1920 in the shape of the much-travelled small steamer *Amelia* (341grt, 1894), owned by William Cooper & Son of Kirkwall. Built originally for a Great Yarmouth firm, she had been sold in 1900 to Nova Scotian owners and saw service on the Canadian coast until 1918, when she was sailed back across the Atlantic when much needed tonnage was needed to offset war losses in home waters. Cooper's bought her in March 1920 to carry food and household goods north to their warehouse and carry agricultural products south. This independent service was maintained until June 1940, when it was merged into the North of Scotland, Orkney & Shetland Steam Navigation Company's sailing schedule. *Amelia* is seen here approaching her berth further up the Water of Leith, still in her Cooper colours – she never changed them – in 1951. Reliable as she was, eventually the high cost of coal and old age beat her and she arrived at the breaker's yard at Charlestown, Fife, on 24 May 1955.

LEITH & KIRKWALL SHIPPING CO.

(WM. COOPER & SON, OLD DOCK, LEITH, and HARBOUR, KIRKWALL)

GENERAL CARGO SERVICE   *STEAMER "AMELIA"*

LEITH to KIRKWALL, Every FRIDAY

KIRKWALL to LEITH (via ABERDEEN) Every MONDAY

Telegrams: "COOPER, KIRKWALL"   Captain P. S. COOPER,   Telephones: KIRKWALL 19
"EXPRESS, LEITH"   Lloyd's Agent for Orkney   LEITH 36951

Opposite below: Coast Lines of Liverpool ran services round the northern coastline of the United Kingdom and their vessels called at Leith. *Eastern Coast* (1,223grt, 1922) was often found sailing between Liverpool and Leith, calling at such ports as Belfast, Stornoway and Aberdeen on the way. Sold to Bermudan owners in 1954 and to South African owners a year later, she went to the shipbreakers after running ashore in 1964.

Above: Another short-lived short-sea sailing was that of *Barjama* (837grt, 1924) between Leith
and the Faroe Islands, a group of islands governed by Denmark, lying to the north-west of the
Shetland Islands. As the Glasgow-registered *The Marquis*, she was purchased by the Leith
businessman Charles Mauritzen in 1940, who employed her to carry supplies to the isolated
islanders, and to bring back much-needed fish to Scotland. Renamed *Barjama* in 1945, she
survived this hazardous route until 25 January 1952 when she ran aground in a blizzard off
Kirkebobaes in the Faroes and became a total loss.

Above and below: From the mid–1930s Coast Lines began to replace steamers with motor vessels. From that time the Liverpool–Leith sailings (via the north of Scotland) were operated by vessels with accommodation for twelve passengers. One of these vessels was *British Coast* (889grt, 1934), built by Henry Robb Ltd of Leith. She was sold to Newfoundland owners in 1964 and became a total loss after running aground in the Turks and Caicos Islands on 14 July 1981.

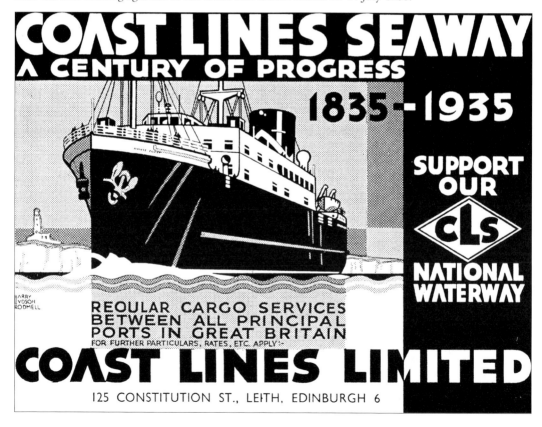

three

Northern
Europe

From early times Leith had a considerable trade with northern European ports. One of the companies involved was the Leith, Hull & Hamburg Steam Packet Company. The Company can trace its beginnings back to 1843 and the formation of the Leith & Hull Steam Packet Company. Later services were extended to Hamburg and it was these beginnings that led to the formation of the Leith, Hull & Hamburg Steam Packet Company in 1854. James Currie and his brother, Donald, joined the firm in 1862 and soon established a large building programme, with the intention of opening up routes to Copenhagen, Stettin, and other North German and Baltic ports. Later they introduced passenger ships to the Copenhagen and Hamburg sailings. By 1914 the company was operating thirty-nine ships, twenty of which were lost in the war. Trade recovered and in 1939 there were twenty-seven ships in service; however, by 1946 only nine remained. In 1940 the company changed its title to the more appropriate name of Currie Line. Trade never recovered after the war and gradually the fleet dwindled away, the company being absorbed by the Anchor Line (part of the Runciman Group) of Glasgow in 1969, and all 'liner' sailings to northern Europe from Leith ceased in September 1971.

Opposite above: The newly completed *Inverawe* (2,185grt, 1914) was not so fortunate as she had arrived at Cronstadt, Russia, on 3 August 1914, and had then found herself trapped in the Baltic. She 'escaped' and eventually arrived at London in August 1917. *Inverawe* was sold to Estonian owners in June 1935 and in 1941 (on the occupation of Estonia by Germany) was transferred to the Honduran flag. She sprang a leak off Corfu on 18 February 1960 and later sank.

Weimar (1,590grt, 1890) was built for Hamburg passenger sailings. She departed from Hamburg on 31 July 1914, in time to escape detention on the outbreak of war, and was the first British ship to arrive at Hamburg after the war on 15 September 1919. She arrived at Stockton for breaking up in December 1933, after forty-three years' service.

During the 1920s the company acquired secondhand tonnage. One of these vessels, purchased in December 1927, was from William Thomson & Company of Leith which was renamed *Shetland* (1,846grt, 1921). A typical Baltic trader with holds capable of taking long lengths of timber, she is seen berthed at Leith on 1 April 1938. She was sunk in an air attack off Cape St Vincent, Portugal, while on passage from Lisbon via Gibraltar to Belfast on 23 June 1943.

A new pair of passenger ships were built for the Leith–Copenhagen service in the 1920s. *Horsa* (979grt, 1928) was one of this pair. During the Second World War she ferried supplies to the Faroe Islands and Iceland, and resumed sailings to Copenhagen in 1946. Sold in November 1955 to Glasgow owners, she survived until she arrived at Antwerp for breaking up on 26 June 1959.

The year 1932 saw the introduction of a series of new steamers with accommodation for twelve passengers. *Courland* (1,325grt, 1932) was the first of these vessels and was employed on the Leith–Hamburg sailings. She was torpedoed and sunk by U37 in the North Atlantic while on passage from Lisbon via Gibraltar to London on 9 February 1941, with the loss of all her crew of thirty.

During the Second World War, companies which had suffered war losses of a specialist type of vessel could have new ships built if granted an appropriate licence. Currie's were granted such a licence for several Baltic-type vessels, one being *Iceland* (2,896grt, 1943). Built at Dundee, she remained in service until she was sold to other owners in July 1956. She was eventually broken up at Eleusis, Greece, in November 1979.

To replace war losses (twelve vessels were lost) after the Second World War, vessels were acquired from the Ministry of War Transport in 1946. One of these was renamed *Highland* (1,876grt, 1944). When trade was poor in European waters in the 1950s, she was chartered to sail between New York and the Caribbean, until she was sold to Dundee owners in March 1959. She was broken up in Italy under the Greek flag in September 1969.

Three sister ships were built in Germany to operate the cargo-only sailings to Copenhagen and Hamburg/Bremen. *Courland* (877grt, 1956) was the first of these ships and was employed on the German services. All three ships were laid up at Leith when Currie's withdrew from operating sailings in September 1971. *Courland* was sold in October 1971 to Lebanese owners and by 1995 had been deleted from the Register.

Finland (877grt, 1956) was the second of this group, and was also employed on the German sailings. She too was laid up at Leith in September 1971 and was sold to other Lebanese owners. She was gutted by fire off Sicily and sank on 27 July 1981.

four

The Low
Countries

George Gibson & Company were founded in 1844 and moved into steam in 1850. The company's principal trade was to the Low Countries (Holland and Belgium) and this expanded over the years with regular sailings from Leith to Rotterdam and Antwerp. On the opening of the Suez Canal in 1869 they operated steamers in the Far East trade for a few years but withdrew in 1880. Passenger sailings to Rotterdam and Antwerp were introduced in 1883 and further ports of call, such as Amsterdam, Ghent and Dunkirk were added to their cargo sailing lists. In January 1920 an amalgamation took place with James Rankine & Company, who had been operating sailings from Grangemouth and also to the Low Countries since 1854. Latterly trade involved a considerable tonnage of vegetables and fruit, and to reduce the cost of handling, certain vessels were modified to carry the goods on pallets and subsequently in containers. The company branched out into the carriage of liquefied gas and chemicals and some of the dry cargo vessels were converted to carry this type of cargo. With the contraction of both the dry cargo and gas/chemical market, an approach was made in February 1972 to the Anchor Line of Glasgow (who had already absorbed the Currie Line) and agreement was reached that George Gibson & Company would be merged with this group. With the conversion of the last dry cargo ships to liquefied gas carriers in 1968, the container services were maintained by chartered tonnage.

One of the passenger steamers was *Eildon* (1,329grt, 1905), which introduced sailings between Rotterdam and Grangemouth. She could accommodate first-class passengers as well as a large number of emigrants, who at that time were moving from eastern European countries to North America via Glasgow. War took her to strange waters and she was wrecked near Ushant, north-western France, while on passage from Workington, Cumberland, to Nantes, France, with a cargo of iron and steel on 4 May 1915.

The amalgamation of Gibson's with Rankine's brought with it the passenger steamer *Grangemouth* (1,560grt, 1908). As Gibson had lost all their passenger vessels in the war, she took over Gibson's Leith–Antwerp sailings. She was to retain the Rankine funnel colours until sinking off the river Humber after a collision with a trawler on 23 March 1939.

A standard vessel laid down for the Shipping Controller was acquired and completed as *Dryburgh* (1,352grt, 1919). She was employed on sailings to Antwerp and Ghent as her ample hold capacity was most suited to the carriage of jute from Belgium to Dundee. Despite her low speed (8kts) she continued to sail between Antwerp and Leith when war broke out, but on 11 November 1939 sank in the Humber estuary after striking the wreckage of the Danish liner *Canada* (11,108grt, 1935).

Three vessels provided with extensive cargo-handling gear were built in 1920. One was *Crichtoun* (1,125grt, 1920) which was employed on the Leith–Antwerp sailings. She was sunk by an E-boat off Lowestoft on 19 March 1945, while on a voyage from Leith to London with a general cargo – twenty-two of her crew of twenty-five were lost.

In 1936 a decision was made to convert the fleet to diesel propulsion, and delivery was taken of *Eildon* (1,447grt, 1936). She was mainly employed carrying coal from Scotland to the south of England and Europe. During the war she was requisitioned as a cased petrol carrier, visiting Iceland and the Mediterranean, as well Normandy. Sold in October 1966 to Greek owners, she was broken up in 1980.

Before: *Quentin* (500grt, 1940) was one of several small motor vessels to join Gibson's during the war period. She was employed as a cased petrol carrier during the D-day landings in the summer of 1944. She finally made her first commercial sailing to Amsterdam in March 1946. When Gibson's obtained a long-term contract to carry liquid ammonia from Heysham, Lancashire, to Belfast (later also to Dublin) in 1965, it was found most economical to convert the twenty-five-year-old vessel rather than construct new tonnage.

After: *Quentin* was fitted with the necessary tanks in her single hold by Henry Robb Ltd at Leith, and came into service as a tanker in September 1965. She arrived at Sheerness, Kent, for breaking up on 12 February 1976.

The policy of changing over to diesel propulsion, begun in 1936, continued after the war. *Crichtoun* (873grt, 1946) was delivered by Grangemouth Dockyard and was employed mainly on the Antwerp sailings. When the dry cargo trade became less economic *Crichtoun* was sold in September 1965 to Canadian owners. She sank off Cape Race, Newfoundland, on 22 April 1991 after sustaining ice damage.

The slightly larger *Cardrona* (1,525grt, 1947) was delivered by the same yard a year later. She was employed carrying wheat from the Low Countries to the United Kingdom, timber from Archangel, northern Russia, to Belgium and steel from Belgium to Scotland. She was sold to Greek owners in March 1968 and was broken up at Perama, Greece, in March 1971, after suffering severe grounding damage.

Abbotsford (1864grt, 1955), another shelter-deck vessel built at Grangemouth, took over the Antwerp sailings. In 1959–60, because of the decline in trade, she was sent out to Canada to operate in the Great Lakes. *Abbotsford* was sold in June 1963 to South American owners in June 1963. She sank after being driven on the mole at Cristobal, Panama, on 13 January 1981.

Sailings between Dunkirk and Portugal were introduced on the acquisition of the motor vessel *Lanrick* (570grt, 1957). When Gibson's won a contract in 1969 to carry propylene from the River Tees to Grangemouth, *Lanrick* was withdrawn from service and converted to a tanker in Holland. She arrived at Hartlepool for breaking up on 27 May 1982.

Ettrick (1,144grt, 1959) was built with no cargo handling gear as only palletised cargo was to be carried. She could also carry twelve passengers. She was modified in 1966–67 to carry 40–50 containers when sailings from Grangemouth to Rotterdam were introduced. When further contracts to carry butane were won in 1968, *Ettrick* proceeded to Holland, where she was lengthened and converted into a tanker. While loading butane at Augusta, Sicily, in September 1971, a fire broke out, resulting in repairs costing £60,000. Sold to Panamanian owners in November 1972, she finished up in a breaker's yard in Greece in November 1985.

When Gibson's obtained a contract to carry ethylene from Middlesbrough to Rotterdam in 1966, two tankers had to be bareboat chartered to meet this commitment. One boat was *Traquair* (694grt, 1966). She was transferred to Anchor Line Ltd in December 1977 but because she was now technically obsolete, she was sold to Panamanian owners in September 1979. After developing a leak in the engine room, she foundered 400 miles south of Mobile, Alabama, while on passage to New Orleans on 14 February 1981.

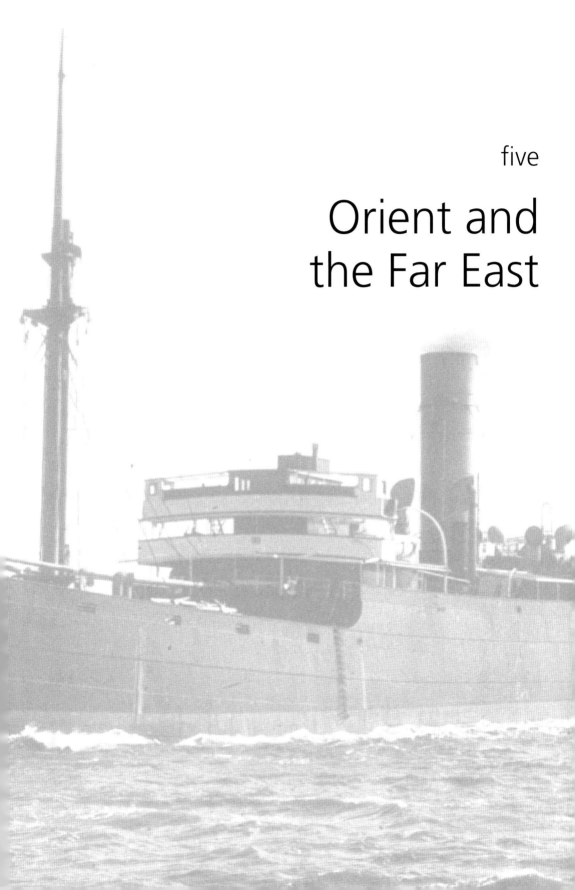

five

Orient and the Far East

William Thomson & Company, ship owners since 1847, introduced steamers to their Far East trade in 1871. But their sailing ship traditions died hard and even though steam was the principal motive power, the steamers were partly rigged so that they could make port in the event of a breakdown. The company was advertised at this time as 'The Clipper Line of Steamers' when the first steamer named *Benledi* (1,557grt, 1871) was placed on the sailings, and was subsequently well known as 'The Ben Line'. After the war the company was re-organised and the formation of The Ben Line Steamers Ltd took place in 1919. Although only two of the Far East steamers had been lost in the conflict, there was an urgent need to replace the older tonnage by the purchase of second-hand vessels and the building of new ones. As years went by, with coal from Leith no longer a staple cargo, the port latterly saw less and less of Ben Line ships, with loading for the East being undertaken at Hull, London or Continental ports. Ben Line sold its final ship and withdrew from shipowning in 1992.

One of the early 'Leith Yachts' was *Benalder* (3,044grt, 1895) which saw service with the company until 1919. She then flew the Portuguese flag as *Ganda*, until being broken up in 1929.

Benarty (3,910grt, 1902) was the fourteenth steamer in the fleet but, like her predecessors, retained her yacht-like appearance, though the presence of sails was not obvious. Here, she is sailing down the Thames fully laden for yet another voyage to the Far East. She remained with the company until 1924 when she was sold and became *Antinoe*. After her cargo of grain shifted in the mid-Atlantic she was abandoned at sea on 28 January 1926.

A similar vessel, *Benlarig* (3,921grt, 1904), is on the Thames in light condition, awaiting a berth to load for the Far East. When under requisition by the Royal Navy as a collier, she was reported missing after sailing from Fremantle, West Australia, bound for Colombo, Ceylon, on 2 April 1917. Sabotage was suspected.

Benlawers (3,949grt, 1905) is sailing down the Thames. She is one of six sister ships built by Bartram & Sons, Sunderland, for William Thomson between 1902 and 1907. She was sold to Russia in 1930 and was deleted from the Register in 1959, as it was believed she was no longer afloat.

Benlomond (4,887grt, 1911) was a slightly larger version of *Benlawers*. She survived until 3 March 1932 when she arrived at the breaker's yard at Shanghai.

The last steamer with a clipper bow to be built for William Thomson was *Benrinnes* (4,798grt, 1914). Launched in June 1914 by Bartram & Sons, Sunderland, she survived the war after two torpedoes fired by a U-boat missed her. Sold in December 1937 as *Thorpeness*, she was a blockade runner during the Spanish Civil War. She was bombed and sunk in an air attack at Valencia in the course of this activity on 21 June 1938.

To meet the new era after the war a whole series of ships were built by Charles Connell & Company, Glasgow, including the solid-looking *Benvorlich* (5,193grt, 1919). She served The Ben Line until she was sunk in an air attack in the North Atlantic on 19 March 1941.

Further ships built by Connell joined the fleet, including *Benreoch* (5,818grt, 1921). She served The Ben Line until she was sold to Japan for further trading on July 1951.

Benarty (5,800grt, 1926) traded successfully to the Far East until 10 September 1940 when she was captured by the German raider *Atlantis*, the ex-merchant ship *Goldenfels* (7,438grt, 1911) in the Indian Ocean, and later sunk by time bombs.

Benvenue (5,920grt, 1927) was also lost through enemy action when she was torpedoed and sunk some 500 miles west of Freetown, West Africa, on 15 May 1941.

Benmohr (5,920grt, 1928) also suffered the same fate in this area on 5 March 1942. As seen here, she had the misfortune to run ashore at Prawle Point, Devon, in February 1931, but survived to sail again.

Whereas only two ships had been lost by William Thomson & Company in the First World War, a total of fourteen were lost in the Second World War. *Bencruachan* (5,920grt, 1928) was one of these, being mined and sunk off Alexandria, Egypt, on 5 July 1941.

Ten ships were built by Charles & Connell of Glasgow between 1919 and 1930 for Ben Line Steamers Ltd. *Benwyvis* (5,920grt, 1929) was the seventh of this group and, like others, finished up as a war loss when she was torpedoed and sunk by U105 north of the Cape Verde Islands on 21 March 1941.

Charles Connell & Company started to deliver a series of larger ships between 1944 and 1969, the first being *Benlawers* (7,804grt, 1944). A fine-looking ship, she served the company for twenty-four years before arriving at Kaohsiung, Taiwan, for breaking up on 20 February 1968.

During the Second World War, William Thomson & Company were managers of several Liberty Ships on behalf of the Ministry of War Transport. After the war the company bought several of them to make good the gaps in the fleet and gave them *Ben* names. One of them was *Ammla* which was renamed *Bendoran* (7,252grt, 1944) on her purchase in April 1947. She was sold to Panamanian owners in 1953 on delivery of the new ships ordered after the war.

With the need to be able to carry locomotives and other heavy machinery to the Far East, the Ben Line purchased the heavy lift ship *Empire Athelstan* (7,795grt, 1946) which was renamed *Benalbanach*. When the demand for the carriage of such equipment declined in 1963, she was laid up at Hartlepool and sold back to the Ministry of Transport in November 1965. Under the Panamanian flag, she arrived at Split, Yugoslavia, on 5 December 1975 for breaking up.

Another Liberty Ship, *Salmonier* ex-*Samont* (7,273grt, 1943) was managed by William Thomson & Company from October 1947 on behalf of a subsidiary company, the Salmonier Shipping Company Ltd of St John's, Newfoundland. She was placed on the Ben Line berth as *Benmohr* in December 1949. Sold in September 1951 to Liberian owners, she continued to trade until June 1969 when she arrived at the breaker's yard at Kaohsiung, Taiwan.

six

Paper and
Whale Oil

Christian, a member of the Norwegian family of Salvesen from Mandal, set up business in Scotland as a shipping agent in the 1840s. He quickly prospered and ordered his first steamer in 1879, which was followed three years later by another. Subsequently, the fleet extended rapidly with the acquisition of second-hand tonnage – the company was not to order another new vessel until 1935. The red funnel with a white strip and black top was soon to be seen in many ports around Norway and in the Baltic. When war broke out in 1914, the black top of the funnel had to be changed to blue otherwise the ships would have been sporting the German national colours!

The name Christian Salvesen was also for a long time synonymous with Antarctic whaling. The company first went into whaling in 1904, operating from a small base in the Shetlands. Encouraged by the reports from the Antarctic the company made the decision to enter this new venture in 1907. A base station was established in South Georgia (appropriately named Leith Harbour) and the equipment for this was relocated from a redundant station in Iceland. Over the years a large fleet of whalers was owned, together with their associated factory and supply ships. The company withdrew from whaling in 1963 and also from shipowning in December 1989.

Tana (1,169grt, 1882), the second vessel to be built for Salvesen's, is lying in the river Carron, Grangemouth, awaiting demolition in 1935. Christian's first steamer had unfortunately been wrecked off Holland a few months before *Tana* was delivered. The first voyage for *Tana* in August 1882 was on charter to the British Government carrying supplies to Egypt, where British forces were putting down a rebellion. Subsequently, for over fifty years she traded to Norway and the Baltic.

Another purchase was *Glitra* (2,925grt, 1910) in February 1918, requisitioned as a collier at that time and not released until April 1919. Although a useful steamer, because of the general slump in the early 1930s, she had to be laid up at Swansea in December 1935. Sold in October 1936, she finished up in the breaker's yard at Troon in February 1937.

A Dutch steamer was purchased in February 1924 and renamed *Ailsa* (1,343grt, 1918). She was a useful size for the Baltic trade, carrying coal out and timber back. She was sold to Danish owners in May 1936 and renamed *Reval*, and is seen here under that name discharging a cargo of coal at Hobro, Denmark, in August 1936. She sank after striking a mine in the North Sea on 23 January 1940.

Salvesen's purchased the Aberdeen fleet of J. Cook & Son in 1925. Among the vessels taken over was *Glen Gairn* (904grt, 1922), seen here leaving Granton, bound for Norway with a cargo of coal, having previously discharged a cargo of wood pulp and newsprint. Time-chartered by the Ministry of Transport in November 1940, she was subsequently sold to London owners in April 1942. After several owners and names, she finally sank off Syros Island, Greece, on 8 April 1958 while under the Greek flag.

To replace war losses, the company, like many others, purchased government owned ships. One such vessel was *Empire Patriot* (2,881grt, 1942), previously managed by Salvesen's, which was bought and renamed *Struan* in April 1946. However, her service with the company was relatively short because by the late 1950s the cost of operating a steamer was becoming uneconomic. She is seen here laid up at Leith. To reduce costs she was moved out into the upper Forth off Blackness Castle in 1959. Eventually sold to Syrian owners in 1960, she was broken up at Istanbul in February 1974.

After the Second World War the company started to acquire motor ships. The first such vessel was the wartime-built *Empire Cliff* (873grt, 1940) in September 1945, which was renamed *Marna*. When newer and more modern vessels were delivered to the company she was sold in November 1960 to London owners. When under the Panamanian flag, she sank after a collision off Casablanca, Morocco, on 4 September 1971.

The first of the new breed of motor ships was *Glitra* (992grt, 1952) built for the company at Wallsend, Tyne and Wear. She was to serve the company until July 1969 when she was sold to Somali Republican owners. She foundered at sea whilst sailing from Oran to Avonmouth on 8 June 1971.

The company later ordered six motor ships, which were slightly larger and with their bridge aft. The last of these was *Laksa* (1,323grt, 1960) and she served Salvesen's until they withdrew from the Norwegian trade in 1971. Sold to a Glasgow ship owner in August 1971, she still remains afloat under the Lebanese flag as *Noor Aldin*.

To support the whaling, operation required larger ships, one of these being the Liverpool cargo liner *Politician* which Salvesen's purchased in 1922 and renamed *Coronda* (7,503grt, 1899). She was employed carrying out supplies to the base, returning each year with whale oil and by-products – she was a very smelly ship! She was laid up in the Clyde in October 1945 then went to the breaker's yard at Ghent in March 1946.

As well as supply ships, the company bought tonnage to convert into factory ships to process the catch of whalers. One of these factory ships was *Sevilla* (7,022grt, 1900), converted from a German liner interned in Argentina in 1914 and passed to Great Britain after the war. Purchased in April 1922 she served the company until she too arrived at the breaker's yard at Ghent in June 1949.

Brandon (6,665grt, 1917) was another of the company's supply ships and is seen moored at Leith Harbour in South Georgia. Purchased from the Canadian Pacific Railway Company of Liverpool in February 1928, she was employed in the tramping trade when not required in the Antarctic. She was torpedoed and sunk 150 miles west of Land's End on 8 December 1942.

Over the years Salvesen's owned a large number of whale catchers. The design was basically the same throughout and *Southern Jester* (591grt, 1950) was one of the more modern vessels employed. Purchased from other owners in August 1952, she was sold to Norwegian owners in November 1964 after the company withdrew from whaling in 1963. *Southern Jester* was later converted to a cargo vessel and fitted with a diesel engine, and is still afloat as *Strilhval*.

Whale catchers frequently found they needed assistance in towing the whale carcasses to the factory ship or land station. Salvesen's came up with the solution of converting some wartime corvettes to whale-towing vessels. One of them was HMS *Lotus*, converted for such service at Leith, and renamed *Southern Lotus* (851grt, 1942) in January 1948. She returned to Norway after the 1963 season and was laid up at Oslo until December 1966, when, under tow to the breakers at Bruges, she broke away from her tow and was driven ashore on East Jutland, Denmark, becoming a total loss.

seven

Stone and Cement

The steam coasters of A.F. Henry & MacGregor were a well-known sight in Leith and other Scottish ports between the wars. They first became shipowners in 1907 and initially purchased steam barges to trade from Leith to as far north as Montrose and to Berwick-upon-Tweed in the south. They expanded into coastal trading in 1910, when they took delivery of the small coaster *Kinnaird Head* (910grt). She was sold in 1919 and became *Glas Island* in 1939. She is seen below in 1952, pushing down the Clyde off Dumbarton Rock in a strong westerly breeze. She was broken up in October 1955. Larger vessels were purchased in the early 1920s and they were generally employed carrying road stone to southern English ports, loaded at Inverkeithing on the Forth, or Newburgh on the Tay, or coal loaded at Leith. On the return voyages they carried bagged cement from the cement works on the banks of the Thames, to many ports on the east and north-east of Scotland and in the Northern Isles – they could be seen in such ports as Montrose, Buckie, Inverness, Wick, Kirkwall and Lerwick. Smaller vessels in the fleet were employed carrying coal to Orkney and Shetland, and bringing grain south. In 1941 control of the company passed to the London & Edinburgh Shipping Company, which had lost all its ships by enemy action by June 1941. With the opening of a cement works at Dunbar, East Lothian, in 1963 and the consequent loss of the cement traffic from the Thames, the London & Edinburgh Shipping Company sold their interest to Christian Salvesen Ltd, which enabled them to re-enter the short-sea and coastal trade. The fleet then rapidly expanded with new and larger vessels being added. The Henry & MacGregor black funnel with two narrow white strips was retained until 1976, after which the ships in the fleet had their funnels repainted in Salvesen colours. With the withdrawal of Salvesen's from shipping in December 1989, all the remaining ships were sold.

Most of the early company's vessels were purchased secondhand. *St Abbs Head* (635grt, 1914), seen here entering Tréport, northern France, was acquired from Clyde owners in 1923. She survived the war (although the company lost five ships), and continued in service until steam ships were becoming uneconomical to operate. She arrived at Rosyth on the upper reaches of the Forth for breaking up in December 1953.

Noss Head (438grt, 1921), built for the company, is seen sometime between 1935 and 1939 in the Albert Dock, Leith, loading coal – note the state of her paintwork covered in cement dust. Astern of her is the North of Scotland, Orkney & Shetland Steam Navigation Company's cargo steamer *St Fergus* (390grt, 1913) awaiting her turn to move on to her loading berth on the other side of the dock. *Noss Head* was lost near Gardenstown, Banffshire, from unknown causes on 27 February 1941. *St Fergus* sank after a collision off Rattray Head, Aberdeenshire, on 31 December 1941.

Rattray Head (496grt, 1921) was a vessel purchased in 1929 from Belfast owners. She did not survive the war after she was attacked and sunk by aircraft eight miles east-north-east of Aberdeen on 5 April 1941.

Holburn Head (489grt, 1925) was purchased from Mersey owners in 1930 and gave the company twenty-four years' service until 1954. She is seen here proceeding down the Thames with a full load of bagged cement. She was sold back to other Mersey owners and was finally broken up in Holland in August 1961.

Barra Head (671grt, 1930), acquired in 1931, served the company for thirty years with no major incidents reported – quite an achievement in a trade that called for the vessel to put into many small ports, such as Montrose and Lossiemouth, which are difficult to enter in bad weather. She finally went to the breakers at Grangemouth in August 1961.

As well as coasters of 500–600 tons, Henry & MacGregor also owned several small vessels of about 300 tons. *Denwick Head* (265grt, 1923), seen in the Albert Dock Basin, Leith, was acquired from Cardiff owners in 1933. *Denwick Head* was sold to Glasgow owners in 1946, and broken up in July 1955. The General Steam Navigation Company's steamer *Groningen* (1,205grt, 1928) can be seen loading on the London berth.

The smart looking coaster *Oriole* (488grt, 1921) was purchased from the General Steam Navigation Company of London in 1935 and renamed *Cantick Head*. She too survived the war and was sold to Mersey owners in 1955 when steam was rapidly being replaced by diesel. She was finally broken up at Dublin in October 1960.

To expand into the coal trade, the company purchased three rather larger ships between 1947 and 1949. Two of these were wartime engines-aft steamers, one of which was *Rattray Head* (1,066grt, 1943). She continued to trade for the company until she was sold to Italian owners in 1960, finally arriving at Savona, Italy, for breaking up on 10 July 1973.

The company bought its last steamer in 1955. This was the Swedish *Ingwi* (2,006grt, 1947) which was renamed *Denwick Head*. She was the first foreign-built ship and the last steamer in the fleet, and was sold in 1963, being broken up at Antwerp in August 1969.

The modernisation of the fleet from steam to motor ships commenced in 1952. Instead of buying second-hand tonnage as in the past (with the one exception of *Denwick Head* already mentioned), new ships were ordered. The first of these, ordered from the local yard of Henry Robb Ltd, was *Marwick Head* (1,786grt, 1952), designed not only for the coal trade but also for trading further afield such as the Baltic, north Russia and even the Great Lakes in North America. *Marwick Head* was sold in 1969 when larger ships were required for the coal trade. She is still trading under the Greek flag as *San Nikolas*.

As the older steamers which could enter Inverkeithing to load stone were sold, it became necessary to built replacement motor vessels to meet this commitment. The first of these was *Dunnet Head* (749grt, 1953), again built by Henry Robb Ltd. She continued to trade until sold to Canadian owners in August 1965. She dropped out of the Register in 1991.

A second motor vessel capable of loading at Inverkeithing and entering the smaller Scottish ports, *St Abbs Head* (647grt, 1956), was built, but this time at a yard in Holland. Salvesen decided to withdraw from this trade and sold her to Indonesian owners in August 1967. She is still trading as *Saffora 1*.

Further vessels for the coal trade were introduced, one of which was *Cantick Head* (1,591grt, 1958), built on the Clyde. She saw service in the fleet for thirteen years before being replaced by still larger tonnage. *Cantick Head* was sold to Greek owners and later passed through the hands of several more owners. She sank on 14 November 1982 off the Isles of Scilly, once again under the British flag, after developing a list on a passage to Whitehaven from Casablanca, Morocco.

Rattray Head (1,600grt, 1965) was fitted with a bridge-controlled engine and alternating current – innovations for a British coaster. She was sold to other British owners in 1973 when she became too small for the bulk coal trade, which now was concentrated on north-east English ports. She became a total constructive loss in Galway Bay, Eire, after running aground on 29 January 1975.

A pair of larger coastal bulk carriers were ordered in 1967, one being *Dunvegan Head* (4,396grt, 1968). When coal traffic was poor, she was employed on the carriage of phosphates from Casablanca to Leith or Aberdeen. The Central Electricity Generating Board took her (and others in the fleet) on long-term contract to carry coal to the Thames and renamed her *Fort Point*, although management was retained by Salvesen's. She was laid up at Hartlepool in November 1986 on the introduction of three 14,000-ton colliers by the Board, and was sold to foreign owners the following year. She is still trading under the Panamanian flag as *Shanti*.

eight

Coal for
the South

The coal trade between south-east Scotland and the south of England employed many vessels owned by various private companies and public utilities. Both Leith and Granton saw a continual stream of empty colliers arriving from the south to load up 'black diamonds' for consumption by householders and the public utilities, such as the power stations and gas works. Many of the latter at one time operated their own fleet of vessels. Other well-known and long-established collier companies were William Cory & Son, Hudson S.S. Company, William France, Fenwick & Company, the South Metropolitan Gas Company, and the London Power Company. When power stations were built further up the Thames a type of collier that could pass under various bridges en route was called for; thus the 'flat iron' collier was developed. This vessel had to have a low profile, and masts and funnel had to have the capability of being lowered. Leith or Granton did not normally see many of the early vessels of this type, but as their numbers began to increase in the 1930s they were frequently loading coal at both Leith and Granton.

Top: Dagenham (2,178grt, 1919) was typical of the class vessel employed, with four large holds and engines amidships. Owned by Hudson's, she carried coal south from Scottish and north-eastern English ports for thirty-six years. The decline in coal production and the economics of operating a coal-burning ship sealed her fate and she was sold to Panamanian owners in 1956. However, she was not to serve them for long, as she foundered off the Turkish Black Sea coast on 29 November 1957.

Above: A representative vessel of the modernised fleet of France Fenwick is *Moorwood* (2,034grt, 1945). By the time she was built the trade now favoured a vessel with her engines aft, as this gave a better trim north when in ballast. She was sold to other collier owners in 1960 and later became a sand barge in Holland.

William Cory & Son had been in the trade for many years and in the 1920s were replacing their older tonnage with larger and more modern ships, including *Corsea* (2,764grt, 1921), seen proceeding down the Thames on her way north for another cargo of coal. As can be seen at the stern, when sailing light the propeller lost some of its effect. Because of the change in trading conditions, she was sold to Finnish owners in 1953, and arrived at Antwerp and the breaker's yard in January 1958.

Corminster (1,707grt, 1928) was another of Cory's fleet. She too continued in the trade for thirty years before being sold to Greek owners in 1958. By this time coal production in Scotland was rapidly declining and North Sea petroleum gas was replacing gas previously produced from coal. She arrived for breaking up at Split, Yugoslavia, on 23 November 1967.

Cory's changed to vessels with engines aft quite early on. An example is *Corfirth* (1,803grt, 1934). Although seen in ballast, her propeller is still well submerged. As the demand for coal declined, so did Cory's fleet and *Corfirth* was sold to Greek owners, and registered in Monrovia in 1959. She arrived at Savona, Italy, for breaking up on 28 May 1967.

The South Metropolitan Gas Company operated the *Camberwell* (1,577grt, 1924). Built to service their gas works sited on the Thames, she passed to the South-Eastern Gas Board in 1949, when the industry was nationalised. She finally arrived for breaking up at New Waterway, Holland, in July 1958.

John Hopkinson (1,314grt, 1932), a 'flat iron' owned by the London Power Company. On the nationalisation of the industry in 1948 she was transferred to the ownership of the Central Electricity Generating Board. She was broken up at Grays, Essex, in 1959.

Steam 'flat irons' were still being built after the war, and *Sir Alexander Kennedy* (1,714grt, 1946) of the London Power Company is a good example. She remained in service until she was broken up in Belgium in 1968.

Fulham Power Company owned a series of 'flat irons'. *Fulham II* (1,596grt, 1936), seen loading in the Imperial Dock, Leith, in 1936, was one of a pair of ships built to supply the new power station located in Chelsea, the furthest point up-river that colliers ran to. She supplied the station with coal for twenty-four years, finally arriving at Sunderland for breaking up on 28 June 1960.

Fulham X (1,759grt, 1948) was the last 'flat iron' ordered by the Fulham Power Company before the company was nationalised and became part of the Central Electricity Generating Board. Seen in a loaded condition going up the Thames off Greenwich in 1951, one can image how it must have been like on her in any sort of North Sea storm – she was already half submerged! She was also the third vessel in the fleet to be propelled by an oil engine, which no doubt accounted for the fact that she survived the breaker's torch until her arrival at Blyth on 30 July 1970.

nine

Coasting
Traders

Many small coasters were employed in carrying coal and wooden barrels north, especially during the herring seasons around the turn of the twentieth century. There was also a thriving trade in carrying coal north from the coalfields in Scotland and the North East of England to fill the bunkers of the many trawlers based in Aberdeen. When coal was still the main fuel for heating and cooking, large quantities of it were stockpiled at such ports as Aberdeen, Inverness, Kirkwall and Lerwick to satisfy the needs of householders in the many towns and fishing ports along the Moray Firth coastline, and in Orkney and Shetland. For many years this trade remained in the hands of sailing vessels, but gradually steam took over.

One of the early coasters was *Matje* (284grt, 1890), owned by the Leith & East Coast Shipping Company from September 1905. Carrying coal north and fish products south proved not to be cost-effective at that time, due to competition and a series of accidents to the vessel. Matters were brought to a head when *Matje* ran ashore west of Kirkwall on 19 June 1906, resulting in the company being forced into administration on 17 December 1906. *Matje*, sold in August 1907, served on the west coast of the United Kingdom until she was broken up on December 1936.

Other companies and other ships entered – and left – the trade. The fish-curing firm George Couper & Company of Helmsdale, Caithness, also owned several ships, one being *Naviedale* (383grt, 1906). She and other vessels were employed moving fish products to markets, both in the United Kingdom and northern Europe. *Naviedale* was in service from 1932 until broken up in May 1956.

Another regular visitor to load coal was the Aberdeen-registered motor vessel *Ferryhill* (567grt, 1946), seen leaving Aberdeen bound south to load yet another cargo in 1960. Previously owned at Newcastle under the name of *Moray Firth*, she was acquired by the Aberdeen Coal & Shipping Company in 1959. She remained in this trade until coal was transferred to the railway in the 1970s. She went to the breakers in 1972.

Other Leith owners entered the coal and grain trade from 1946 onwards. W.N. Lindsay Ltd operated several tired (and often rusty) steamers, not only trading to the north but also to the south. *Mistley* (485grt, 1920) was purchased from Liverpool owners in April 1952. She sank on 19 June 1957 after striking the Reefdyke Rocks off North Ronaldsay, Orkney, while on passage from North Ronaldsay to delivery coal for the inhabitants of Fair Isle.

On occasions Lindsay's bought a better class of tonnage. *Roseneath* (1,366grt, 1949), previously a collier, passed to the Associated Portland Cement Manufacturers Ltd when the coal trade declined in 1959. When Scotland's first cement works came on line and the need to ship cement north by sea ceased, she came on the second-hand market and was quickly snapped up by Lindsay's in 1962. She was broken up in Holland in April 1968.

Although most of the early ships owned by Lindsay's were steamers, they branched out into motor ships in August 1957 when they acquired *Karri* (354grt, 1938) – seen leaving Kirkwall in 1960 – which proved very suitable for the grain trade. She was sold ten years later to Greek owners and foundered fifty miles south of Toulon, after springing a leak when the engine failed on 19 May 1977.

Another motor vessel acquired by Lindsay's was an ex-Army stores ship. Re-named *Rosemarkie* (499grt, 1939) in 1958 after conversion to a cargo ship, she served Lindsay's until she arrived at Inverkeithing for breaking up on 12 August 1968.

The locally owned coaster *Enid Mary* (582grt, 1921) is discharging grain in the Edinburgh Dock, Leith, in 1954. She was initially owned by Laverock Shipping Company in 1953 and by Enid Shipping Company from 1955. When the economics of operating a single steamer became dubious, she was sold to Liverpool owners in 1956 and finally arrived for breaking up at Preston on 14 June 1960.

Cement was often discharged at Leith by vessels registered in Glasgow and London, supplementing that landed by the vessels of Henry & MacGregor. J. Hay & Sons Ltd of Glasgow employed such vessels as *The Duke* (820grt, 1927) in the trade for many years. She was to serve the company for a total of thirty-four years before arriving at the breakers at Grays, Essex, on 8 February 1961.

J. Hays & Sons acquired a wartime-built steamer to replace war losses in 1946. They named her *The Monarch* (1,059grt, 1946). She is seen sailing down the Water of Leith in 1954, having discharged yet another load of bagged cement. She was sold to Lebanese owners in 1962 and broken up at Eleusis, Greece, in September 1968.

William Robertson, also of Glasgow, was another owner with a large fleet of steamers which called at Leith to discharge cement. *Turquoise* (570grt, 1924) was typical of the vessels in that fleet. She was stranded near Maryport, Cumbria, on 5 January 1950 and, after being refloated, was repaired and sold to Castle Coasters Ltd of Leith, and renamed *Tynecastle*. She traded for them until she arrived in tow at New Waterway, Holland, for demolition in November 1959.

Another Glasgow company involved in the trade was John Stewart & Company. The names of their ships all had the prefix 'Yew'. They initially owned steamers and *Yewdale* (987grt, 1949), seen approaching a berth at Leith, was of the new generation of motor vessels now coming into service. Sold in 1969 to Greek owners, she was unfortunately stranded at Île de Croix, France, on 28 March 1971 and broke up.

Motor ships of the London owner F.T. Everard & Sons were often seen at Leith. They had a large fleet of motor ships by the late 1930s. A typical vessel of that company such as *Summity* (554grt, 1939) is seen at Leith. *Summity* was sold to Greek owners in 1966 and is still trading as *Panagia M.*

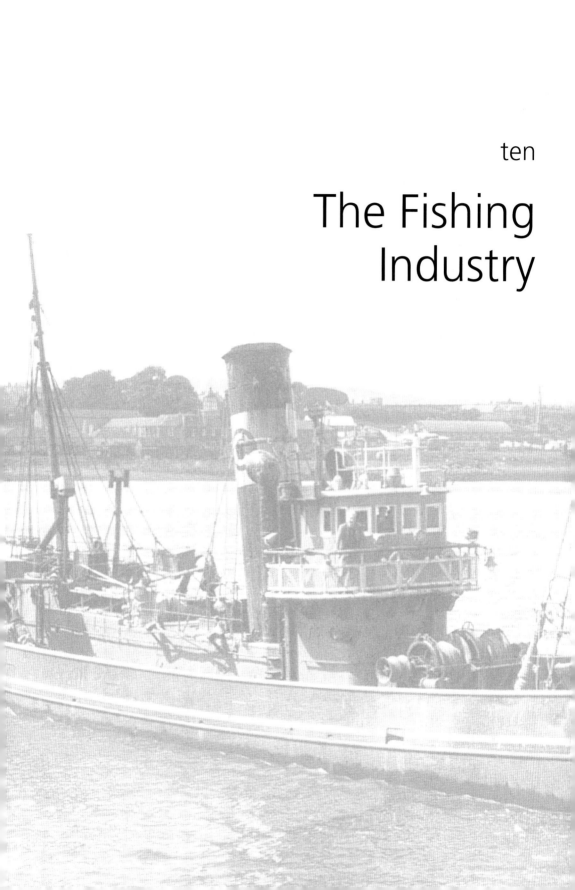

ten

The Fishing Industry

Granton has been a fishing port since 1885. One of the principal trawler owners of the port was Thomas L. Devlin. He began to build up a fleet of steam trawlers in 1890 and by 1900 had sixteen in service. A further series was built from 1903 to 1915. He was to build only one new trawler after that, in 1930, otherwise depending on the purchase of second-hand tonnage to maintain his fleet. One such acquisition was an ex-Admiralty trawler in 1920, which was renamed *Madden* (237grt, 1917). She is seen moving to a berth on the west side of the Middle Pier in 1959. The West Breakwater was then being used to bunker trawlers. *Madden* was broken up at Granton by Malcolm Brechin in December 1962, after forty-five years' service, which is a tribute to the good workmanship of her builders, Hall, Russell & Company of Aberdeen.

A view from the Middle Pier of the *Thomas L. Devlin* (211grt, 1915) sailing for the fishing grounds in 1959. She had been acquired from Aberdeen owners in 1925 and came to an untimely end when she was wrecked on May Island, at the entrance to the Firth of Forth, on 29 December 1959.

Another well known trawler owner was William Cairnie. *Lord Rivers* (266grt, 1935), an oil-burning vessel built in Germany, was acquired from Hull owners in 1950. She returned from her last fishing trip on 28 June 1962, and arrived at Grangemouth for breaking up in October 1963.

Diesel engine trawlers came on the scene in the 1950s, with more and more of these craft taking over from the steamers, some of which had given their owners more than forty years' service. *Granton Falcon* (272grt, 1956) owned by William Cairnie is a typical example of this type of vessel and is seen departing for the fishing grounds in 1968. By 1970 the fishing industry was in crisis and all the local trawler owners were bought up by larger groups. *Granton Falcon* was sold to British United Trawlers Ltd in 1970. She arrived in tow at Middlesbrough for breaking up on 10 August 1977.

The Glasgow-registered but Granton-based trawler, *Barbara Paton* (273grt, 1957), owned by the Ardrossan Trawling Company, is leaving Granton on her way to the fishing grounds in 1968. She was sold to William Liston Ltd of Leith in 1970, and absorbed as *Arctic Explorer* into the Boyd Line Ltd of Grimsby in 1972, part of the Associated Fisheries Group. While laid up, she sank in Cattewater Harbour, Plymouth, on 10 February 1979.

The older established trawler owners were gradually going out of business by the early 1960s, but others came on the scene in their place. One was Joe Croan, who owned *Granton Merlin* (235grt, 1960), seen coming into the Middle Pier. She was absorbed into the fleet of British United Trawlers Ltd in 1970, and in 1978 renamed *Umberleigh* when she became a off-shore safety vessel. It is believed she was classified as a yacht in 2002.

eleven

Coastline
Protection

Lighthouse Tenders

The Commissioners of Northern Lights have been responsible for providing and maintaining navigational aids round the long coastline of Scotland since 1786. In that year the construction of four lighthouses was authorised. To service the lighthouses and light buoys scattered round the coastline from Berwick-upon-Tweed in the east to the Isle of Man in the west, sailing vessels were initially employed, but in 1839 the first steam tender was brought into service. Over the years the number and size of these tenders increased, largely depending on the duties they had to perform. During the 1980s automation of the lights commenced, and by 1988 all lighthouses around the Scottish coastline were no longer manned – instead their performance was 'supervised' from a control room in Edinburgh. With now only routine maintenance to carry out, and no monthly keeper reliefs to perform, the number of tenders was gradually reduced and, by March 2003 there was only one depot at Oban, the others (Granton/Leith and Stromness) having been closed, and two tenders in service.

One of the smart yacht-like tenders was the twin-screw *May* (242grt, 1899). Seen at her berth in the south-west corner of Granton, she had wooden decks, and smart mahogany upperworks. She 'serviced' the lights in the Forth area for thirty-seven years, going to the breakers at Bo'ness, West Lothian, in January 1938, by then named *Dundrenan* to allow the name to be used by a new ship.

Traditionally the Commissioners have always owned a vessel named *Pharos*, which as well as carrying out reliefs, could accommodate members of the Board on inspections. The seventh vessel of this name, *Pharos* (921grt, 1909), built by William Beardmore & Company on the Clyde, was another twin-screw yacht-like vessel. Berthed at the Middle Pier, Granton, she was capable of serving at any of the Commissioners' three bases. During August each year when she was on her 'inspection' trip, she could be seen anywhere around the Scottish coastline paying visits to various lighthouses. By 1954 she was becoming expensive to operate, so was replaced by another vessel of the same name, and went to the breakers at Charlestown, Fife, in September 1955.

Another product of the Beardmore yard was *Pole Star* (750grt, 1930). Slightly smaller than *Pharos* and without accommodation for the Commissioners, she was stationed at Stromness, Orkney, until 1961, when as *May* she moved to Granton for her last four years of service. She was broken up at Glasgow in February 1965.

The Commissioners' first motor vessel came into service in 1937. The second *May* (491grt, 1937) took the place of the earlier vessel of that name. Berthed at Granton like her predecessor, she remained on station until 1962, when as *May III* she was laid up at Leith pending disposal. Sold in March 1963 for gas/oil research surveying, she passed through several hands before arriving at Bo'ness, West Lothian, for breaking up in October 1977.

The eighth ship to be named *Pharos* (1,712grt, 1955) was built at Dundee and took over the duties of her predecessor at Granton that summer. Not looking so much like a yacht, she nevertheless had superb accommodation and was just as comfortable. By the 1960s lights were starting to be automated and there was less of a need for tenders, with the use of helicopters to carry out maintenance work now being quite common. While other tenders in the fleet could be fitted with a helicopter pad, this was not possible with *Pharos* because of her extensive upper works aft. By 1988, with no regular reliefs to perform as all the lights had become automated, the fleet was reduced, and *Pharos* was sold to act as a 'mother ship' to a flotilla of yachts operating in the Caribbean.

Fishery Protection

In the 1880s, with the rapid development of trawling, a stricter control of the sea fisheries round the Scottish coast was required. The Fishery Board for Scotland (later to become the Department of Agriculture & Fisheries for Scotland) was created in October 1882 to enforce the regulations, investigate methods of fishing, and to monitor the fish stocks in the sea areas adjoining Scotland, in the North Sea, between Scotland and the Faroe Islands, and on the west coast from the Scottish border out to the lonely Atlantic sentinel of Rockall. Initially, fishing limits internationally extended just twelve miles from the coastline and the patrolling of this area was shared with the Royal Navy. Within a few years, however, the Department built a fleet of fishery cruisers which were permitted to fly the blue ensign on which the Fishery Board Badge was superimposed. The vessels were given grey hulls which gave them the appearance of a warship, and were based at either Leith or Greenock on the Clyde. The Department also manned research vessels which carried out investigations into the level of fish stocks and means of improving methods of trawling.

One of the early inshore patrol vessels was the Leith built ex-steam yacht *Vigilant* (134grt, 1886), purchased in 1894. She remained in service until broken up in 1936.

It was not until the commissioning of *Norna* (457grt, 1909) that a vessel capable of steaming long distances and staying at sea in all weathers came on station. Normally based at Leith, she is seen coming off patrol in 1953. Always smartly kept and looking 'navy-like', she was taken out of service in 1960 and arrived at Troon for breaking up on 11 March 1960.

When the need for additional tonnage was required after the Second World War, two Admiralty coal-burning trawlers were acquired in 1946. One was renamed *Longa* (462grt, 1944), seen in the Albert Dock, Leith. Known locally as one of the 'Smoky Joes' because of her smoke-making abilities, she remained in service until arriving at Inverkeithing, Fife, for breaking up in November 1973.

The Department always had a research vessel available with the task of investigating the various methods of fishing, and monitoring the state of domestic fish stocks. *Explorer* (862grt, 1955), originally laid down as a Greenland trawler, was completed for the Department for this purpose. She was sold for breaking up and arrived at Inverkeithing, Fife, in June 1984 but was acquired for preservation.

Although the fleet was being changed over to diesel propulsion, an oil-burning trawler was commissioned as a patrol vessel in 1971. Seen lying in Edinburgh Dock, Leith, she was the *Switha* (573grt, 1948), built as a research vessel on the lines of a Greenland trawler. Her end was unfortunate: returning to Leith she ran ashore on a reef to the south-east of Inchkeith in the Firth of Forth on 31 January 1980. Her crew were taken off by helicopter but salvage was found impossible and her remains lie there to this day.

The prototype of a new class of patrol vessel, *Jura* (892grt, 1973) was commissioned into service and is seen lying at Stornoway, Outer Hebrides, in 1978. She was based on the experience of *Switha* and designed to achieve a service speed of 16kts. Such was her performance that the Admiralty 'borrowed' her for a period in 1975 to assess her capability to serve on off-shore duties in the protection of gas and oil field rigs in the North Sea. As a result the Admiralty ordered seven such vessels based on her design (designated by the Royal Navy as the 'Island' class).

Above: With a need for a type of craft suitable to patrol inshore, the fast patrol launch *Morven* (70grt, 1983) was introduced. With a maximum speed of 24kts, she is much more likely to be able to catch any offenders in shallow sea lochs and confined waters.

Previous spread: With the experience gained from earlier vessels, *Sulisker* (1,250grt, 1981), a vessel with twin-screws, more powerful engines to increase performance, and fitted with stabilisers to give her crew greater comfort in heavy weather, was brought into service. She was the first vessel to be built specifically to undertake patrols up to the 200-mile limit.

twelve

Harbour Tugs

Towage services at Leith and Granton were for many years provided by the Leith Salvage & Towage Company. As well as salvage work, the company performed towage and docking duties within and around Leith and Granton. The bulk of the salvage work was undertaken by two vessels named *Bullger* and both vessels were well known around the eastern side of the United Kingdom. While paddle vessels were best suited to acting as stern tugs in docking operations, more powerful vessels were needed for their greater pulling power, and this was provided by screw tugs. The Leith Salvage & Towage Company went into voluntary liquidation in 1953 and Leith Dock Commission took over the towage responsibilities. Until 1956 all the tugs had been purchased second-hand, but that year, for the first time, an order was placed for two new tugs fitted with Kort nozzles to improve their handling in confined areas. To replace the last of the steam tugs in 1967, 'water tractors' fitted with Voith Schneider omni-directional propellers were brought into service. When ports and harbours were rationalised in 1968, the control of these facilities within the lower Forth area passed to the Forth Ports Authority. In 1982, when the Authority obtained a contract to maintain 'stand-by' tugs to cover tankers loading at Braefoot Bay, west of Burntisland, Fife, larger and more powerful tugs with firefighting capabilities were built. All five tugs in the fleet of the Forth Ports Authority in 1983 were transferred to the subsidiary company, Forth Estuary Towage Ltd.

The salvage vessel *Bullger* (364grt, 1883) had been in service with the Royal Navy as HM Tug *Traveller* from 1885, until purchased by the Leith shipbuilders, Hawthorns & Company, in May 1920. She was reconditioned by them before being transferred to the Leith Salvage & Towage Company, in which they held an interest, and being renamed *Bullger*. She carried out many salvage tasks until 20 January 1924, when she unfortunately struck rocks at the entrance to Anstruther Harbour, Fife, while attempting to refloat a trawler ashore near that harbour. A storm broke up the hull on 12 March 1934.

This advertisement shows the second tug named *Bullger* (304grt, 1907). Built as *Cartmel* and previously employed at Barrow by the London, Midland & Scottish Railway, she came into service in May 1934. While escorting a salvaged steamer to the Tyne she struck a mine and sank near Warkworth, Northumberland, on 16 March 1941.

The iron paddle tug *Flying Fish* (169grt, 1882) was purchased from Bo'ness owners in 1920. Here, she is sailing out of the Imperial Dock basin at Leith; judging by her smart condition, she is just out of dry dock. She was sold to Middlesbrough owners in 1947 and broken up at Gateshead on the river Tyne in January 1951, after sixty-seven years afloat.

Oxcar (252grt, 1919) was purchased from Dutch owners in January 1926 and proved to be a very versatile and useful tug, if rather smoky. She is seen here towing a vessel into the Imperial Dock Lock at Leith in 1953. She was broken up at St Davids-on-Forth, Fife, in the summer of 1967, the steamers in the fleet having been replaced by diesel-powered vessels.

The two-funnelled tug was bought from German owners in February 1929 and named *Herwit* (254grt, 1904). She is seen moving – with the assistance of the paddle tug *Gunnet* – the London & Edinburgh Shipping Company's steamer *Royal Archer* into dry dock in the mid-1930s. *Herwit* was broken up at Inverkeithing, Fife, in March 1947.

As well as attending launches, there was also the mundane task of towing dumb barges out to sea to dump their spoil. *Gunnet* (180grt, 1896), purchased from Teeside owners in July 1933, frequently had this task, and is seen returning to Leith with a barge in tow on 26 July 1937. She remained in service until broken up in 1952, after fifty-six years' service.

On return to peace in 1945, the company went about replacing their older tugs. A Clyde screw tug was purchased in June 1946 and renamed *Mickry* (172grt, 1920) to replace the forty-two-year-old *Herwit*. *Mickry* was one of the last two steam tugs to serve Leith, and went to the breakers at St David's-on-Forth, Fife, in 1967.

A small harbour tug *Kalisco* (62grt, 1917) had been employed for many years at Leith by Kalis & Sons of London who were constructing the new breakwaters to form the Western Harbour. When that work was completed in 1956, Leith Dock Commission bought her as a useful addition to their fleet. She went to the breakers in January 1959.

Shortly after the Leith Dock Commission took over the tug fleet the Leith Salvage & Towage Company in 1953, consideration was given to replacements. Two motor tugs were delivered in early 1958. One was *Martello* (65grt, 1957) seen passing outward through the Imperial Dock lock in 1961. She was sold in 1977 and is still in service.

The second tug delivered in 1958 was the larger *Craigleith* (175grt, 1958), which is seen moving a vessel away from a berth in the Western Harbour. She was sold to south of England owners on becoming surplus to requirements in December 1979. Sold to Canadian owners in 1984, she has since been converted into a yacht.

Gunnet (143grt, 1967) was one of these vessels fitted with Voith Schneider propellers. She is seen in the Western Harbour. When more powerful tugs with firefighting capabilities were required, she was sold to Lowestoft owners in March 1991, and is still in service, registered at Waterford, Eire.

With the need to provide safety and firefighting cover for tankers loading at Braefoot Bay Oil Terminal, Fife, the larger tug *Oxcar* (250grt, 1978) was delivered in 1978. She had twice the bollard pulling power of *Gunnet,* delivered around nine years earlier. *Oxcar* is seen lying in the Albert Dock awaiting her next assignment.

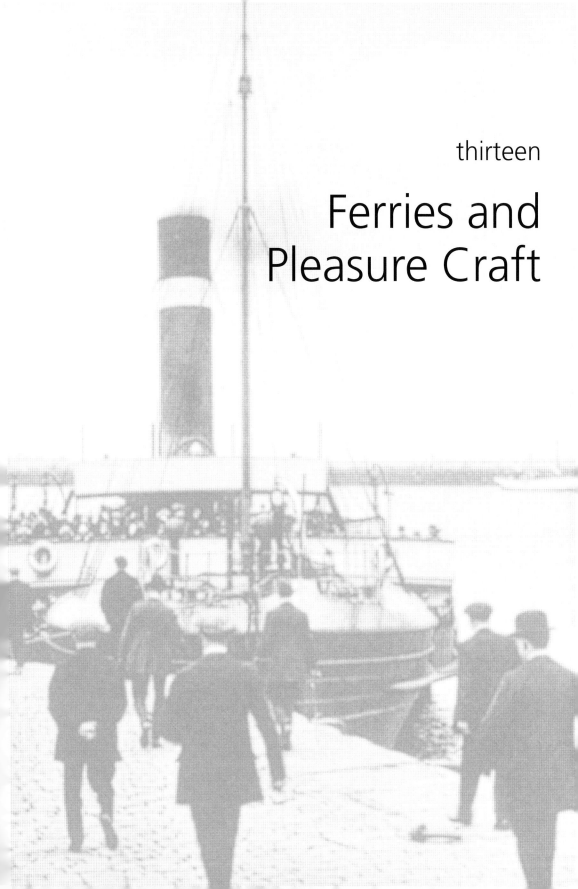

thirteen

Ferries and Pleasure Craft

Ferries

A steam ferry service between Granton and Burntisland, on the north shore of the Forth, had been introduced in 1845. Until the completion of the Forth Bridge at Queensferry in 1890, a train ferry was also in operation. *William Muir* (412grt, 1879) was built for the North British Railway Company to cope with the increased passenger traffic on the opening of the Tay Bridge in May 1878, and originally had two funnels. She carried across the Forth the passengers who joined the fateful train which plunged into the Tay on 28 December 1879. Re-boilered and re-engined in 1910, she came back into service with a single funnel. *William Muir*, seen at the ferry slip at Granton, with her promenade deck already well packed, awaits her last few passengers.

William Muir is approaching her berth at Granton in the mid-1930s. Except for a short spell as a minesweeper between January 1917 and July 1919, she served the crossing for fifty-eight years. She went to the breakers in March 1937.

Changeover day dawns on 3 March 1936. The smartly painted *Thane of Fife* pulls the rather care-worn *William Muir* off the ferry slip at Granton to allow her to take over the service.

The twin-screw *Thane of Fife* (457grt, 1910) took up the ferry service in March 1937. Built as *Snowdrop* for service on the Mersey, she was bought in October 1936. To allow vehicles to be carried, part of her forward saloon was removed. She is seen sailing out of Granton in 1937, bow first – with twin screws she could turn within the harbour. The ferry service was suspended in March 1940 and *Thane of Fife* was then employed by the Royal Navy at Rosyth Dockyard. The ferry service was never resumed after the war and *Thane of Fife* was broken up at Passage West, Cork, in 1948.

The re-introduction of a ferry service to Burntisland was proposed in March 1949, with a half-hourly service being provided by four converted wartime landing craft. Scheduled to commence on 1 August 1950, the service eventually started in April 1951, and was operated by Forth Ferries Ltd. *Flora Macdonald* ex-LCT (4) 895 (469grt, 1942) and *Bonnie Prince Charlie* ex-LCT (4) 673 (469/1942) are lying at the ferry slip at Granton prior to entering service in 1951. Alongside is the pleasure motor vessel *Ulster Lady* (128grt, 1947) – also owned by Forth Ferries – which acted as a passenger overflow vessel during summer weekends.

Glenfinnan (ex LCT (4) 1048 (469grt, 1942)) is seen entering Granton with a good load of vehicles. In November 1952 the service was suspended and the company went into voluntary liquidation. Laid up at Granton until 1954, she and her sister ships were sold to owners in Goa.

Pleasure Craft

Pleasure sailings from Leith were introduced by the Galloway family in the 1860s, initially employing tugs that they owned on sailings from Leith to Aberdour, just west of Burntisland in Fife. As demand grew, purpose-built steamers were acquired and sailings extended to other places on the Forth. Sailings on the Forth were never to become so popular as those on the Clyde, mainly because the Forth had fewer piers at which the vessels could call, and fewer islands to sail round. The area suffered at times from strong north-easterly winds, which made pleasure sailing less attractive than on the calmer waters of the Clyde. While a cruise round the Forth Bridge was popular from the late 1880s, other than the pier at Aberdour and the harbour of Kirkcaldy, the only places that the steamers could land passengers (other than by small boat) were Portobello (a suburb of Edinburgh) from 1871, North Berwick, East Lothian from 1888 and Elie, Fife, from 1889. A majority shareholding in the company was acquired (with M.P. Galloway being retained as manager) in 1891 by the North British Railway (who ran the ferry service between Granton and Burntisland) and further steamers were then added. The outbreak of the First World War and the death of M.P. Galloway himself in November 1913, heralded the end of pleasure sailings on the Forth for a time.

One of the early purpose-built ships was *Lord Morton* (220grt, 1883). She was the first ship in the fleet to have saloons both fore and aft. In August 1917 she was purchased by the Admiralty and converted to Hospital Carrier HC 7 and sent out to the White Sea, north Russia, to support British forces fighting in the area. She was blown up, to prevent her falling into the hands of the Bolsheviks, on 29 September 1919.

Another paddle steamer that Galloway's employed on excursions was *Tantallon Castle* (393grt, 1899), capable of a speed of 15kts. She was somewhat 'tender' for the waters of the Forth and was sold in May 1901. She was to see service in the south of England for some years before being sold to Portuguese owners in 1912.

Pleasure sailings were reintroduced on the Forth in the early 1920s, employing tugs as before. It was not until 1927 that a purpose-built steamer came into service again, when the Grangemouth & Forth Towing Company purchased the Clyde steamer *Isle Of Skye* (211grt, 1886) and renamed her *Fair Maid*. Brought into service from Leith on 5 June 1927, her sailings were limited to calls at Aberdour, a seaside resort near Burntisland in Fife, and Kirkcaldy, with trips to view the Forth Bridge. She is seen here entering Leith with the East Breakwater in the background. On the outbreak of the Second World War all excursion sailings were withdrawn and in 1940 *Fair Maid* moved to the Clyde as a decontamination vessel. She never returned to the Forth and was broken up in 1945.

Competition for excursion passengers on the Forth came on the scene in 1934, when a Hull company, Redcliffe Shipping Company Ltd, placed the paddle steamer *Cruising Queen* (302grt, 1903) on a berth at Leith. Originally a ferry on the Humber, she had served as a transport in Mesopotamia during the First World War, and had been hit several times by shell fire – she sported the patches to prove it. By then she was an old and tired vessel and after just one season went to the breakers.

Flushed with the initial success of the *Cruising Queen*, the same owners bought the West Highland paddle steamer *Fusilier* (280grt, 1888) in July 1934, and based her at Granton. She is seen at her berth at Middle Pier, Granton, ready to take an afternoon sailing, on 14 August. She was a beautiful little steamer but was not built to take the short sharp seas which were met at the entrance to the Firth of Forth, and remained on station for just two months, after which she was sold to Welsh owners and moved to quieter waters. She was finally broken up in October 1939.

The venture was obviously a success because the same company sent the doubled-ended ex-Humber ferry *Highland Queen* (508grt, 1912) north in 1935. She returned for the 1936 season but sailed out of Granton. The 1936 season was so poor that in August she was moved to East Anglia to try her luck there. It was no better and she went to German shipbreakers in December 1936.

Excursions on the Forth returned in the summer of 1947 when a Kirkcaldy businessman purchased the Scarborough motor ship *New Royal Lady* (250grt, 1938). Renamed *Royal Lady* (seen here in the eastern harbour), she commenced sailings from Granton on 1 May, but expectations were not achieved. In November she was sold to the General Steam Navigation Company of London, to operate cruises through London Docks. In 1957 she was sold to Maltese owners and as *Imperial Eagle* sailed between Malta and the island of Gozo until laid up in February 1994. She was finally scuttled as an artificial reef off Gozo in July 1999.

CRUISING ON THE
FIRTH of FORTH

P.S.
"HIGHLAND QUEEN"

ALL SAILINGS FROM GRANTON PIER

(WEATHER, ETC. PERMITTING)

Teas and Refreshments	DANCE MUSIC	Fully Licensed (Except Sunday)

DATE	AFTERNOON at 2.30	EVENING at 7.30
Monday, 22nd June	BLACKNESS CASTLE and FORTH BRIDGE	THREE INCHES
Tuesday, 23rd June	LARGO BAY and FIFE COAST	FORTH BRIDGE
Wednes., 24th June	ABERLADY BAY and FIDRA	KIRKCALDY BAY
Thursday, 25th June	FIDRA, to view BASS ROCK	FORTH BRIDGE
Friday, 26th June	KIRKCALDY BAY and FIFE COAST	THREE INCHES
Saturday, 27th June	FIFE COAST and LARGO BAY	MYSTERY CRUISE
Sunday, 28th June	ABERLADY BAY and FIDRA	FORTH BRIDGE

EVERY AFTERNOON at 2.30 p.m.—
FARE—ADULTS, 2/- ; JUVENILES, 1/-
EVERY EVENING at 7.30 p.m.—
FARE—ADULTS, 1/6 ; JUVENILES, 1/-

PARTIES CATERED FOR UP TO 750 PERSONS

A handbill advertising sailings of *Highland Queen* from Granton, 1936. The Saturday night late cruises sailed at half speed and were very popular as the bar on board remained open until entering the harbour just before midnight, thus giving the thirsty nearly two hours' extra drinking time!

Granton Harbour, from the railway embankment which is now demolished, at its junction with the Eastern Breakwater. In the background one of Ropner & Company's (of West Hartlepool) large vessels is loading coal at the outer berth on the Western Breakwater. In the foreground the Devlin trawler *Commodore* (133grt, 1891) is identified by her registration number GN 33. She remained with Devlin's until she was sold in 1924, only to founder twelve miles off Barnes Ness, East Lothian, on 26 May 1925. The two-funnelled paddle steamer is the Northern Lighthouse Board's *Pharos* (574grt, 1874), obviously laid up after being replaced by the new vessel of the same name in 1910. *Pharos* was sold and sailed for Glasgow on 11 November 1911. The date of this picture, therefore, must be between early 1910 and November 1911, when both vessels would have been in Granton.

Index to Ships

Other local titles published by Tempus

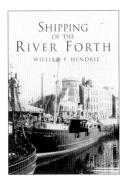

Shipping of the River Forth
WILLIAM F. HENDRIE

For thousands of years the River Forth has been used by man. From Stone Age shell middens to the Roman port at Cramond, there is much evidence for man's use of the river and its estuary. From the fishing harbours along the Fife coast to the ports of Grangemouth, Leith and Granton, as well as the naval bases at Rosyth and Port Edgar, the maritime history of the Forth is covered here. Using over 200 illustrations with detailed captions, William F. Hendrie takes us on a tour of the river and its shipping.
0 7524 2117 4

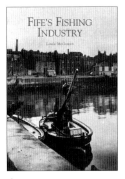

Fife's Fishing Industry
LINDA MCGOWAN

Fishing has always been a mainstay of Fife, a county where nowhere is far from the sea. Linda McGowan charts the growth of the industry through photographs from the archive of the Scottish Fisheries Museum, located in Anstruther. The images concentrate on the East Neuk but other parts of the county are included. The days of hundreds of boats in harbour are long gone but many people in the county still make a living from the sea.
0 7524 2795 4

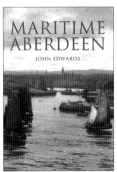

Maritime Aberdeen
JOHN EDWARDS

From fishing boats to ferries, from clipper ships to liners and from oil rig support vessels to the city's history of shipbuilding, all aspects of Aberdeen's rich maritime heritage are shown here in this unique collection of images from Aberdeen Maritime Museum. They show principally the work and ingenuity of the people of Aberdeen who, through their maritime enterprise, developed and sailed some of the finest ships in the world.
0 7524 3218 4

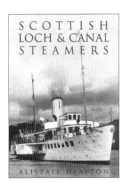

Scottish Loch and Canal Steamers
ALISTAIR DEAYTON

Within the pages of *Scottish Loch & Canal Steamers* are over 200 images of the myriad ships that have sailed on Scotland's canals and lochs. From the *Fairy* and *May Queens* on the Forth & Clyde Canal to the *Queen of the Loch* on Loch Tay, as well as Loch Lomond's many steamers, nearly every passenger vessel that has sailed for commercial gain on Scotland's lochs and canals is illustrated here.
0 7524 3170 6

If you are interested in purchasing other books published by Tempus, or in case you have difficulty finding any Tempus books in your local bookshop, you can also place orders directly through our website

www.tempus-publishing.com